INTRODUCING THE MEDIEVAL

FOX

INTRODUCING THE MEDIEVAL
FOX

PAUL WACKERS

UNIVERSITY OF WALES PRESS

2023

www.uwp.co.uk
British Library CIP Data

A catalogue record for this book is available from the British Library
ISBN   978-1-78683-988-6
eISBN   978-1-78683-989-3

The right of Paul Wackers to be identified as author of this work
has been asserted in accordance with sections 77 and 79 of the
Copyright, Designs and Patents Act 1988.

Designed and typeset by Chris Bell, cbdesign
Printed by the CPI Antony Rowe, Melksham

To Kenneth and Hety Varty,
dear fellow fox hunters and
lifelong friends

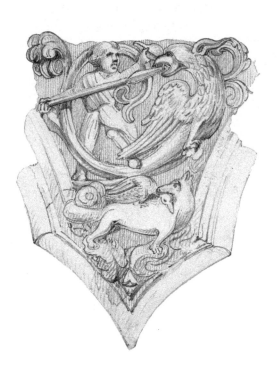

SERIES EDITORS' PREFACE

THE UNIVERSITY OF WALES PRESS series on Medieval Animals explores the historical and cultural impact of animals in this formative period, with the aim of developing new insights, analysing cultural, social and theological tensions and revealing their remarkable resonances with our contemporary world. The series investigates ideas about animals from the fifth century to the sixteenth, and from all over the world. Medieval thought on animals preserved and incorporated a rich classical and mythological inheritance, and some attitudes towards animals that we might consider as having characterized the Middle Ages persisted up to the Enlightenment era – and even to the present day.

Diane Heath and Victoria Blud
Series editors

CONTENTS

PREFACE

A VOLUME ABOUT the fox should be an easy choice for every series about animals because foxes play an important role in almost all human cultures. They are a symbol for and a way of reflecting on the properties, the possibilities and the problems of human ingenuity, with all its different aspects: cleverness, astuteness, guile, ruse, deceit and deception. This is certainly true for the major medieval cultures of Western Europe. We find foxes everywhere and in many different forms; for instance, in texts such as Bible commentaries, encyclopaedias, hunting manuals, fables and epic stories, and in images like miniatures, frescoes, stained-glass windows and misericords, among others. This abundance implies that an introduction like this cannot be complete in any sense, so I have not strived for completeness but have tried to give a clear overview of the main aspects and to present a reliable guide to useful information for those who want to discover more on their own.

The idea for this book came from Diane Heath and I thank her for inviting me to write it. Many people helped me in producing it: Alex Pluskowski, Richard Trachsler and

Baudouin van den Abeele let me profit from their expert knowledge; Diane Heath and Vicky Bludd provided meticulous and helpful editorial commentary; and Sarah Lewis (University of Wales Press) was always there for removing practical problems. I am very grateful to them all.

Although I have worked almost fifty years as a professional on fox stories, many aspects of this book were new to me. I was originally trained as a literary historian, and although I widened my perspective during my career regarding other text types, art history and iconography, I had never thought about subjects such as the behaviour of real foxes, the fur trade, the fox hunt or using some of the fox's body parts for medical purposes before I started writing this book. I learned much by the writing of it and I enjoyed the process. I hope that reading it has the same outcome.

LIST OF
ILLUSTRATIONS

INTRODUCTION

BIOLOGISTS DISCERN more than twenty types of fox. They are, however, cautious when describing their properties and their behaviour because foxes tend to do unexpected things, are not very particular about their food and adapt easily to new circumstances.[1] Hence, they are considered elusive animals. In Western Europe, the dominant fox species is the *vulpes vulpes*, the 'normal' red fox. Although biologists are cautious in their remarks about foxes, the general idea about their behaviour is strong and has existed for a very long time: a fox is cunning, sly and always tries to gain some advantage. An expression of this idea is the proverb 'When the fox preaches, beware your geese'. This modern proverb may be found in many European languages and was already in use in the Middle Ages.[2] It is an indication that the relationship between human beings and foxes has been a long one and that some human opinions on that beast are fairly stable. There are many differences, however, between medieval views on the fox and modern views. This book will describe how foxes were seen and used in medieval religion, in medieval scholarship and how the medieval ideas about foxes shaped a plethora of fox stories, some of which are still very much alive today.

However, cultural ideas about foxes are at least partly determined by their natural behaviour, so we must start with some remarks on the natural fox in the Middle Ages.

THE NATURAL FOX

The medieval landscape may be divided into three parts. The first is the part cultivated by man. This consists of cities, villages and other places where men live, and the ground around them that is used for farming and keeping animals. This settled area grew during the Middle Ages, but even at the end of that period it was far smaller than it is today. Very large parts of Western Europe were wilderness in the Middle Ages. This wilderness may be divided into two parts: the near wilderness and the deep forest. Men went regularly into the near wilderness and while they did not cultivate it they knew it reasonably well, obtaining materials (e.g., wood, plants and fruit) from it and letting some of their domesticated animals use it. The deep wilderness, however, was largely unknown and seldom trodden by man. Cattle and fowl belonged to the cultivated part, and wolves and bears to the deep wilderness. The fox was at home in the near wilderness. As foxes easily adapt to different circumstances, they would have probably been common, but this cannot be proven with absolute certainty. There are, however, indications of widespread fox populations and of human awareness of the behaviour of individual foxes and fox families. A clear indication of human awareness of foxes is found, for instance, in Anglo-Saxon placenames.[3] Among the placenames in Britain that were certainly used during Anglo-Saxon times, there are almost 100 that refer to foxes or badgers. These names show that both species are most often linked with holes or pits (e.g., Foxhole, Brockhall). This makes sense because both species live in dens, badgers habitually and foxes for a large part of the year. On the other hand, these placenames very often associate badgers with woods (e.g., Brockenhurst), but link foxes with hills (e.g., Foxhill) or open spaces in woods. This also is understandable because badgers prefer to live in forests, while foxes tend to choose a more varied landscape offering different types of food – these names therefore point to an awareness of foxes and their behaviour.

With this in mind, however, we do not find attempts to tame or domesticate foxes (but see pp. 35–6). On the contrary, the fox was seen as vermin, mainly because he stole fowl from farms. Most farms were small and kept only a few farm birds: a cock, some chickens, perhaps a few geese. The loss of even one of these was severe, so it is natural that the fox was seen as a pest for farmers and was hunted. But these attempts to kill the fox are unlikely to have entirely prevented a grudging admiration for his slyness. In any case, such grudging admiration seems to be the background for many stories about him, which we will encounter further on in this book.

Ways to hunt foxes will also follow later (see the section about hunting manuals). Yet, what were the possible reasons for hunting foxes? There seems to be three reasons to hunt foxes. The first has already been mentioned: to protect local farmyard fowls. The second is to use his body parts. The third is for fun or sport. The fox is not caught easily, because he is a sly animal, and this makes it interesting to hunt him. Hence, aristocrats hunted foxes not for utilitarian ends but mainly for amusement.[4] But in medieval society everything that could be used was used, including the fox.

Fox meat smells very strong and is mostly considered inedible. Some medieval sources even state that fox meat is mildly poisonous, an idea that is unsupported by modern biology. A hunting manual says that fox fat helps to strengthen animal sinews, which were used as cords or strings and, according to encyclopaedic or medical texts, some fox parts can be used as medicine.[5] The fat or marrow is good for cramped nerves; fox blood is good for stones in the gallbladder or kidneys; the bile helps to cure problems with sight and hearing. Some of the described remedies may seem more like magic to us; for instance, when we read that wearing a ring or a brooch containing the tongue of a fox provides protection against epilepsy. However, this modern distinction between medicine and magic did not exist in the Middle Ages, both were considered ways to influence nature. We cannot determine with certainty that these written recipes were used in practice, but the fact that we also find them in medical treatises suggests that they were more than just theoretical knowledge. And these ideas lived on – for example, we find in the sixteenth century the statement that dried and pulverised fox testicles could be used to cure impotence; and miners and smelters of metal were advised to drink a mixture of fox lungs, scabwort, cinnamon, the juice of muscat grapes, fennel seeds and ground sugar each morning as protection against the bad influence on their lungs of the metal that they worked.[6]

The main product obtained from foxes was, however, their pelt. Fur was commonly used throughout the Middle Ages.[7] It could be used to cover parts of a wall or floor, it could be used for bed covers, hats and clothing. Clothing is by far the most important application and fur was used both as a lining and for decoration. When used as lining it was the best-known way to keep warm in winter. This type of protection was vital, as the only other way of creating warmth in cold periods was by burning wood. Fur trimmings were an important part of the decoration of clothes, demonstrating status or rank, especially when rare or expensive fur was used.

Most of the fur was acquired and used locally, but a widespread fur trade also existed, especially in the later Middle Ages. Traders transported fur that was not needed locally to places where it could be used, and provided customers who could afford the expense with rare and costly types of fur. The skins of rabbits, lambs and sheep were the most typically used for lining clothing. For decoration different colours of squirrel fur were used, as well as the skins of ermine, weasel and the black marten – we find these types of fur mostly in rich and noble circles, while quantitatively and qualitatively fox fur belongs somewhere in the middle. To illustrate the quantitative aspect: between 1227 and 1237 a fur trader in England traded the pelts of 2,174 coneys, 1,016 sheep and eighty-nine foxes; between 1425 and 1441 a trading company transported from Barcelona approximately 500,000 coney pelts, but only 3,000 to 4,000 fox pelts and mere dozens of lynx pelts. In Novgorod (then the centre of the arctic fur trade to western Europe) at the beginning of the fifteenth century there were 195 workshops producing furs – 103 accepted all jobs; thirty-three specialised in beaver fur; twenty-six treated only sheep and goat fleece; seventeen specialised in squirrel fur; and two in fox fur.[8]

Regarding quality, the most remarkable aspect of fox fur in this period is that it was available in so many colours: white from polar foxes; silver and black from the arctic regions; blue from Sweden; yellow from the Iberian Peninsula; bright yellow from the Sahara; and, of course, red and brown from Western Europe itself. Some types were available in reasonable quantities, others were extremely rare. This implies that there is no direct correlation between fox fur and status, as there is, for instance, for ermine and sable, which were used only by the highest nobility. There are indications that rich farmers wore fox fur to show their status, but when the abbot of Saint-Denis (a very important abbey near Paris) decided to wear fur only for warmth and not for status, he did not exclude fox fur.[9] So what gives status to the middle class has a 'neutral' value for the higher classes. In both cases, the fox fur seems to have been obtained locally. The imported fox furs in black, white and blue, were found exclusively in noble circles, and later in very rich circles – they always remained a status symbol.

THE CULTURAL FOX

The most important aspect of the medieval image of the fox is that remarks are very often not about the species but about an individual: Reynard. There is a multitude of stories about this specific fox, who represents everything thought about the whole fox species. Fox stories are told in many languages, so his name has many different forms: Reinardus in Latin; Renart in French; Reinhart or Reynke in German; Reynaert in Dutch; and Rainaldo in Italian.[10] The clearest sign that he represents the species in the medieval mind is that in French the name for the fox changed during the thirteenth century. Originally, the French for fox was *goupil*, but this word was slowly replaced by *renard*. The proper name became the name of a species. Since then, one could (and one can) say in French *le renard Renart* (the fox Reynard). Another sign that the image of Reynard over-lapped with that of the species is the fact that in some fable collections the fox is called Reynard, while normally the characters in a fable are anonymous representatives of species. We see the same phenomenon in *Sir Gawain and the Green Knight*. In that Middle English romance, a fox hunt is described and the prey is indicated not only as 'fox' but also as 'Reynard'.[11] Another sign of Reynard's enormous popularity is that in some Latin and French religious texts we find references to vernacular stories about him that are clearly supposed to be known by the public.

The most distinctive feature of the fox, both as a spe-cies and as an individual, is his cunning. He stays alive, and thrives, not by his force but by his tricks. Hence, he is often called a trickster.[12] This term was developed first in the study of myths from an anthropological viewpoint and has been used since its invention to indicate many dif-ferent types of character, meaning that it should be used with care, but Alison Williams' definition is helpful.[13] For her the term trickster refers to 'a character whose deliber-ate aim is to achieve material gain or psychological victory using wit and deception. For him satisfaction comes from securing the desired prize, and any pleasure in the actual execution is of secondary importance' (p. 1). The fox is very often an ambiguous figure because, as a trickster, he wants to achieve something that he should not have, with a cun-ning that is amazing and sometimes capable of creating

amusing situations. What he wants is negative, but the way that he gets it contains positive elements. This ambiguity returns often.

Sometimes the fox's tricks are 'material' because he uses his body. The best example here is the bestiary fox (see pp. 50–7). When he is hungry, he feigns being dead and thus lures birds of prey to his 'corpse'. When they are near, he grabs them and devours them. Mostly, however, his tricks are verbal. He manipulates his victims by talking and encourages behaviour that leads to their downfall. The famous fable of the fox and the raven illustrates this nicely. The raven has a piece of cheese in his beak. The fox asks the raven whether his voice is as beautiful as his body. The raven opens his beak to demonstrate and the fox gets what he wanted: the cheese.

This attention to verbal tricks in the fox's behaviour links him to humans for whom language is also an important instrument. The fox is often related to the mendicant orders (Franciscans and Dominicans, see pp. 39–40) whose most important task is preaching, to advocates who can manipulate justice by talking, and to the advisers of rulers who determine the fate of the country by the quality of their verbal advice. It is not only in the fox's behaviour that we find these recurrent themes.

The context in which the fox displays this behaviour also has constants. His prey consists in most cases of fowl. In stories, this is usually a cock, while in images it is a goose. His main antagonists are the wolf and the lion. The wolf is presented as strong but stupid and, as the fox is presented as weak but clever, they form an interesting contrast. In the animal epic, the rape of the she-wolf by the fox is given as the reason for this enmity (see p. 94). The lion is the king of the animals. The fox misbehaves continually and very often his victims appeal to the king for recompense. This implies that the fox must often confront the king.

The last point in this section is of a different order. As has already become clear, the fox in this book is referred to as 'he'. Many medieval texts, however, are concerned with the whole species of fox, so many remarks here concern not only the male fox but also the vixen. The 'he' is therefore not determined by sex or gender but by grammar. Fox is a masculine word, hence the use of 'he'. Interestingly, this is mirrored in medieval texts. The word *vulpes* is feminine, so some Latin texts and stories seem, at first sight, to talk about the vixen when they are in fact about the species. The grammatical category says nothing explicit about gender roles. Texts about the fox are not a good entry point for questions regarding gender. The vixen only plays an important role in some fables and in a few stories.

TEXTS AND IMAGES

For the study of the cultural image of the fox in the Middle Ages visual evidence (e.g., murals, sculpture, stained-glass windows and miniatures) is as important as textual evidence.[14] Not only are both representations of the same ideas but the images give us a wider view than the texts can offer alone. In religious and scholarly texts, we find the same ideas about the fox all over Europe. The intellectual, Latin cultural core is the same everywhere and the ideas about the fox are part of that, but the situation is different when it comes to stories, proverbs and adages about the

fox. The extant texts that we have are restricted in terms of time and place. It is from images that we can deduce that some types of story must have been older and were spread over a larger area than we would infer from manuscripts alone. Moreover, images show that versions of stories and sayings must have existed that were not preserved in writing. Furthermore, images sometimes show differences from the stories or explore other elements than those found in the texts.

An example of an image that shows a story must have been older than the remaining written versions is found in a mosaic in the cathedral of Lescar in southern France, near Pau.[15] This mosaic dates from 1130–40. It consists of four parts, one of which shows animals (see Figure 15). Scholars who have studied this mosaic agree that this part refers to a scene from the *Roman de Renart* and although they differ in their identification of this scene, it is clear that the Lescar mosaic is older than the *Roman de Renart* because the oldest parts of that text corpus stem from the period 1174–8. The oral story on which the mosaic was based is likely to be older still because the designer of the mosaic must have assumed that visitors of the cathedral would recognise the story behind his image.

The majority of the stories about the fox came into existence in the southern parts of modern Belgium and the northern parts of modern France – in medieval terms, in the region of the counties of Flanders and Hainaut. In contrast, there are almost no written fox stories from the British isles.[16] But the iconography of the fox is very rich in Britain, so there must have been much orally delivered knowledge about him that has never been written down.[17]

From Italy, we know only one fox story, *Rainaldo e Lesengrino*, which is firmly based on the *Roman de Renart* (see pp. 92–5), but the iconographic material is fairly rich. It shows that regions can have their own themes and that the interpretation of images is sometimes difficult. This can be illustrated by the seven images of a (semi-)dead fox that we find in Italy.[18] The oldest of these stems from the Porta della Pescheria of the cathedral of Modena and is dated before 1135.[19] It shows two cocks bearing a bier on which crouches an animal that is traditionally interpreted as a fox (see Figure 1). Scholars often relate this image to a story from the *Roman de Renart*, which is called *La Mort et Procession de Renart* and which is dated slightly after 1200 – so here again we have an example of an image being older than a corresponding text. However, the relation between that story and this image is problematic.

Figure 1. *Reynard's funeral? Porta della Pescheria, cathedral of Modena, detail. Before 1135. Taken from Houtsma, 'Zeven Italiaanse vossen', p. 238.*

In *La Mort et Procession* the other animals think that Renart is dead and organise his funeral. His funeral procession is large and is described in a very elaborate way, and when the fox unexpectedly comes to life again and escapes, it is from the grave, not from a bier. So, if the image illustrates the story, it has a much smaller procession and a slightly different plot because the resurrection of the fox comes at another moment. This may be explained by assuming that the sculptor knew an earlier, simpler version of the story, with different details, but this can never be more than a hypothesis (and a weak one).

The other six images all show a dead fox carried by two cocks. The dead fox is bound to a pole as a hunting trophy. These scenes are also traditionally interpreted as the fox's funeral, but this interpretation is still more doubtful than in the case of the Modena relief because there is nothing in the images that refers to a funeral. It is equally possible that they represent an example of what art historians call 'images of the world turned upside down'. They show the hunter hunted and caught (see Figure 2). This type of image is often meant for amusement, but all these fox-cock scenes are found as illustrations in churches. This suggests that while it is not impossible that amusement was the aim, perhaps another interpretation is more plausible. Cocks can be a symbol of vigilance and the traditional symbolic meaning of the fox is the Devil. So, this scene could be interpreted as the people catching the Devil and rendering him harmless by being vigilant. Whatever the meaning, these scenes are typical in Italy and this specific representation of the world turned upside down is not found in other parts of Europe.

Figure 2. *Two cocks bearing a caught (and dead?) fox. Mosaic, San Marco, Venice. Seventeenth century, copy of the original from the eleventh century. Taken from Houtsma, 'Zeven Italiaanse vossen', p. 238.*

In the material discussed up until to now we have seen specific, individual differences between texts and images, but we have also seen widespread differences that form a pattern. An example of this is the proverb 'When the fox preaches, beware your geese'. In written material we find only the proverb, but in imagery (e.g., sculpture, frescoes and marginal images in manuscripts) this proverb is developed into a short story: a fox preaches to geese; he tries to grab a bird from his flock; the flock reacts, captures and hangs him. Sometimes this story is presented in a series of images (see Figures 3a and 3b), sometimes we find only the fox hanged. This scene shortening indicates that the public is supposed to already know the 'story'.[20]

Figure 3. *a) A Fox preaching to geese and running away with one of the flock; and b) geese hanging two foxes. Frescoes, Ottestrup Kirke, Denmark, c.1500–25. Photos Hideko Bondesen.*

The example illustrates that we sometimes find elements in images that are absent from texts. As we find many examples of images of geese hanging a fox from Scandinavia and England – countries from which we have almost no stories – this type of image demonstrates that the fox had a wider cultural influence than can be determined based on texts alone.

Another 'structural' difference can be found in the fox that grabs a victim and flees with him, often pursued by a farmer's wife or a group of farmers. In stories the victim is always a cock (see p. 92), in images it is almost always a goose.[21] In the stories the fox tricks his victim by taking advantage of its vanity, and for that reason a cock is considerably more well-suited than a goose. After all, cocks are generally seen as vain and pompous, while geese are considered either silly or clever and watchful – neither property fits with the intrigue of the story. On the other hand, it is easier to make a nice visual composition with a goose because its neck is longer and more slender than that of a cock, so a representation of a fox with a goose flung over his back can be made into a pretty picture.[22] The difference between texts and images may in this case been explained by their different needs.

To conclude this section, I wish to stress two points: it is important to consider the context of an image; and images can have levels of meaning. A good example of the importance of context may be found in the fox with a goose as his victim that we just discussed. When this couple is combined with a farmer's wife holding a distaff, it probably concerns a reference to the story of the fox, fleeing with his prey from the enraged owner (cf. Figures 7 and 11). But on a spandrel in the Elder Lady Chapel of Bristol Cathedral, we see above St George and the dragon and immediately below, a fox bearing off a goose (Figure 4). Here the fox represents the Devil (cf. pp. 33–4). The upper part of the image shows the good destroying the bad, the lower part the triumph of the bad.[23] Five misericord scenes in Bristol Cathedral illustrate part of the story that was introduced in England as William Caxton's *History of Reynard the Fox* (an adaptation of *Reynaerts historie*, see pp. 98–100). They belong together, but this is only understood to someone who knows the story. These five misericords are also a good example of the differences that may exist between a text and its visual representation.[24]

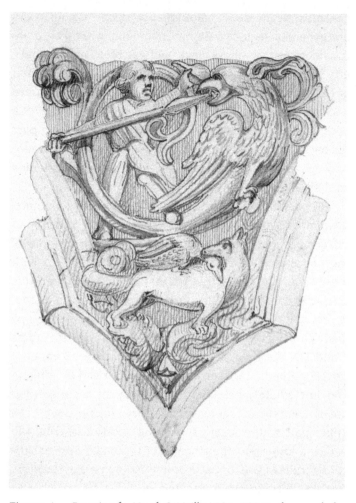

Figure 4.   *Drawing by Hugh O'Neill (1784–1824) of a spandrel in the Elder Lady Chapel of Bristol Cathedral (Bristol Museum and Art Gallery). Above St George fighting with the dragon, below a fox with a captured goose.* © Bristol Museums, Galleries and Archives/ Bequest of William Jerdone Braikenridge, 1908/Bridgeman Images.

That an image may have more than one meaning has already been indicated in the discussion of the Italian images of the two cocks bearing a fox as a hunting trophy. Another nice example may be found in a long-lost fox-preaching scene in stained glass in Leicester Cathedral.[25] We know the image from a sketch made by J. Nichol in 1815 (Figure 5). It shows a fox at a lectern, reading or preaching to three geese. The scene is accompanied by a banderole that originally contained the text 'Testis est mihi Deus, quam cupiam vos omnes visceribus meis' ('God is my witness, how I desire you in my bowels'). An illiterate viewer, unable to read the Latin in the banderole, would be reminded of the popular proverb, 'when the fox preaches beware your geese'. But someone able to read the Latin would see the mixture of pious expression and bad intent and enjoy the joke, while the really learned viewer would

Figure 5. *Stained glass, St Martin's Cathedral, Leicester. Late medieval, now lost. Etching by J. Nichol. Taken from Varty and Wackers, 'A Selective Survey of Visual Representation of Reynardian Literature', p. 225.*

also see that this expression was a deliberate misquotation of the Vulgate version of the words of St Paul to the Philippians (I:8): 'Testis enim mihi est Deus, quomodo cupiam omnes vos in visceribus Jesu Christi' ('God can testify how I long for all of you with the affection of Jesus Christ').

In the rest of this book, texts will dominate but I hope readers will bear in mind that images form an important addition to the information contained in texts. The interpretation of these images is a difficult process for modern scholars, however, because the relationship between images and texts can be hard to determine and because images may have several meanings that are not always clear to us today.

CHAPTER 1

THE FOX AND MEDIEVAL RELIGION

THE BIBLE is the foundation of all medieval religion, so for an understanding of the religious significance of the fox it is important to discover what the Bible says about foxes and what medieval theologians believed these passages meant.[1] There are nine passages in the Bible where a fox is mentioned:[2]

> And Samson went and caught three hundred foxes, and took firebrands, and turned tail to tail, and put a firebrand in the midst between two tails. (5) And when he had set the brands on fire, he let them go into the standing corn of the Philistines, and burnt up both the shocks, and also the standing corn, with the vineyards and olives. (Judges 15:4–5 (4))

> Tobias also the Ammonite who was by him said: Let them build: if a fox go up, he will leap over their stone wall. (Nehemiah 4:3)

> They shall be delivered into the hands of the sword, they shall be the portions of foxes. (Psalm 62:11)

> Catch us the little foxes that destroy the vines: for our vineyard hath flourished. (Song of Solomon 2:15)

> Therefore is our heart sorrowful, therefore are our eyes become dim. (18) For mount Sion, because it is destroyed, foxes have walked upon it. (Lamentations 5:17–18 (17))

> Thy prophets, O Israel, were like foxes in the deserts. (Ezekiel 13:4)

> Jesus said to him: The foxes have holes, and the birds of the air nests; but the Son of man hath no where to lay his head. (Matthew 8:20 [= Luke 9:58]) (cf. Figure 6)

> The same day, there came some of the Pharisees, saying to him: Depart, and get thee hence, for Herod hath a mind to kill thee. (32) And he said to them: Go and tell that fox, Behold, I cast out Devils, and do cures to day and to morrow, and the third day I am consummated. (Luke 13:31–2 (31))

For a modern audience, this collection probably seems fairly disjointed. It refers to the fox as a natural animal that is weak (Nehemiah), has holes (or dens) (Gospels), lives in the wilderness (Lamentations, Ezekiel), is a scavenger (Psalms) and a destroyer when chasing food (Song of Solomon). It shows also that the fox can be used as a metaphor for a sly person (Luke). The medieval interpretation of these quotes, however, gives a coherent image, because medieval theologians thought that the whole Bible had two meanings: the literal meaning and the spiritual (or allegorical) meaning. This spiritual meaning was not based on the human ability to use metaphorical language but on the fact that God used the material things that are mentioned in the Bible as signs for spiritual things.[3] When the quotations above were studied by medieval scholars they all used the same ideas about the 'thing' fox and its meanings and that created a unity that is absent in the modern exegesis of the passages.

The exegesis on the Song of Solomon is extensive because its meaning is obscure. It seems to concern the sensual love between a man and a woman, but in the context of the Bible it must have another, deeper spiritual meaning. In most of the commentaries the little foxes that destroy the vineyard are interpreted as heretics (*haeretici*). Augustine, one of the four Latin Fathers of the Church, explains this as follows:

> Vulpes insidiosos, maximeque haereticos significant; dolosos, fraudulentos cauernosis anfractibus latentes et decipientes, odore etiam tetro putentes.[4]

> The foxes mean the betrayers, especially the heretics; the sly ones, the deceivers who hide themselves in tortuous holes and deceive from there, while they reek with a terrible stench.

These are the foxes that are meant in the Song of Solomon, says Augustine. Catching the little foxes means showing the falseness of their words. Two properties ascribed to foxes are interpreted negatively: that they have holes or dens and that they stink. Living in holes is negative because it is seen

as hiding, as a sign of craftiness and stealth (cf. Figure 6). In the same way, heretics hide their 'wrong' or irreligious ideas beneath truthful and positive-sounding words. Holes are also dark, as are the convictions of the heretics. The stench of foxes is seen as a sign of the depravity of their ideas.

The fox holes and the limping of foxes can also be found in the *Glossa ordinaria*, the 'standard' commentary on

Figure 6. *Fox feigning death to lure the birds and 'foxes have holes'. The Aberdeen Bestiary, (Aberdeen, UB, MS 24), fol. 16r. (England, twelfth century)*

the Bible that we find in many manuscripts, but there they have two distinct elements: 'Vulpes in foves abduntur, et cum apparuerint, numquam directis itineribus currunt, sic haeretici'[5] ('Foxes hide themselves in holes and when they come out, they never walk the straight way, just like the heretics'). Just as foxes hide in holes, so heretics mask their evil intent and when they go among people they spread false ideas, signified by the limping of the foxes. That foxes live in holes and never walk straight are both widespread ideas. That foxes live in holes or dens, we have seen already. The idea that they never walk straight, is found in the high and later Middle Ages and is almost always based on the *Etymologiae* by Isidore of Seville (see pp. 59–60).

The most extensive interpretation of the foxes in the Song of Solomon is probably that of Bernard of Clairvaux (1090–1153).[6] This Cistercian abbot and mystical writer wrote eighty-six sermons on the Song of Solomon and four of them (sermons 63–6) he devoted to the little foxes. He interprets them on two levels: first with regard to monastic life, then concerning the Church. For monks, the foxes mean flatterers, slanderers and especially temptations, or more specifically those vices that appeal to a monk because they seem good (sermon 65, 1). It is fitting that these temptations are called small, not because of their damage but, on the contrary, because they are so unnoticed. It is exactly because they are so unobtrusive that they are dangerous and monks should beware of them. Regarding the Church, the little foxes signify heretics. Bernard compares the heretics of his own time with those of the past, who fought the Church openly because they wanted to defeat it. The heretics of Bernard's own time want to corrupt the Church,

hence they work in hidden ways. Bernard calls them hypocrites. The two interpretations are both based on stealth
and deceit. Bernard uses the fox as an image for what
appears to be good but is in fact bad; for what strives to win
not by an open battle but by ruses and hidden stratagems.

St Bernard's ideas also had an impact on vernacular
commentaries. An anonymous, Middle Dutch, rhymed commentary that is based on Bernard's sermons is interesting
here because it shows how the same ideas can be elaborated in a completely different manner when they are presented in another context.[7] This Middle Dutch commentary
starts with Bernard's interpretation regarding the Church.[8]
His heretics are presented as false Christians. Their behaviour is outwardly correct but they distort the meaning of
Scripture and damage true belief. This is in line with what
Bernard says about the 'modern' heretics, who are hypocrites and work in hidden ways. Next, the Dutch commentary states that there are also clerics who behave in this way
and that they do more damage than laypersons because
they hide their subtle tricks with the help of Scripture so
that laypeople believe them. There are even many members
of religious orders who strive only for worldly goods and get
these by deceiving laypeople (cap. 129, ll. 1–14). The author
says he does not want to write in more detail about this
because he would not have enough parchment or paper, but
he asks all members of religious orders to live according
to their rule and commit no falseness (cap. 129). This distinction between clerics and laypeople and this distrust of
false clerics is completely absent in Bernard's sermons. He
is writing for his fellow monks and not for laypeople as the
author of the Dutch text does.

Bernard's remarks on the little foxes as representing monastic vices are not taken up in the Middle Dutch commentary. In its stead we find remarks on three sins that appear to be good but are actually bad, and that all three are linked to misuse of language:

Drierhande sonden siin
Die slupen comen als vossekiin
Dene is in bedecter reden
Verradenesse uan quader zeden
Die comet mit sueter reden crupen
Ende loselike in den woorden slupen
Die nochtan minnentlike scinen
Dair mede si die siele veninen
Dander is valsche smekinghe
Die bedrieghet ooc sonderlinghe
Menighe blome in den wiingaerde
Der sielen mit groter houairde
Noch is een ander voskiin quaet
Dat der sielen sere scaet
Dats mit loesheit te bedrieghen
Ende in waren scijn te lieghen
Dit siin die uele urucht bederuen
Die die sielen souden eruen
Onsen herc in sine minne. (caput 131, ll. 27–45)

There are three kinds of sin that sneak up on us like foxes. The first [kind] is treachery by concealed language, which results from an evil character. It sneaks up with sweet arguments and in an artful manner it creeps into words which still sound amiable. In this way they poison our soul.

> The second [kind] is false flattery. This too seduces many
> flowers in the vineyard of the soul through pride. There is
> another evil little fox that does great harm to the soul. That
> is by shrewdly deceiving and by lying in such a manner that
> it appears true. These [three] spoil many fruits that the
> soul should inherit from God because of his love.

This passage presents in a nutshell the main elements that
keep turning up when the behaviour of the fox is presented
as an image of human behaviour. The fox acts in ways that
appear fine but are actually evil. Abuse of language plays
a decisive role. All three sins are ways of talking someone
else into doing something that will prove negative for him
or her. This Middle Dutch passage can almost be seen as a
description of the fox's behaviour in literature (Chapter 4,
'The Fox and Medieval Literature').

Two other Bible passages are commented upon regularly, *viz.* Matt. 8:20/Luke 9:58 and Luke 13:32. The foxes in
the first passage are interpreted as heretics, deceivers and
demons. The dominant element in these interpretations
are the holes or dens of the foxes: they signify their hidden ways, their deceit and their deceptions. That Jesus call
Herod a fox (Luke 13:32) is interpreted in a similar way. The
frequent explanation is that Herod stands for cheaters and
deceivers. Another is that Jesus calls Herod 'fox' to indicate that he is a bad ruler who pursues only worldly goals.
And lastly, 'Herod the fox' is seen as a sort of 'archetype' of
the heretics, because he did not want to acknowledge the
divinity of Christ.

Most exegetical remarks are general, but sometimes
more specific interpretations are given. The clearest example

of this is the quotation about the little foxes as sins concerning misuse of language. Another specific interpretation that is relevant in the context of this book is the exegesis of the foxes in the story about Samson in Judges 15:4 in an anonymous Latin commentary.[9] The foxes destroy the fields of the Philistines. They signify bad advocates because on the surface (the head of the foxes) they seem to be divided and to oppose each other, but their tails are bound together because in secret they are connected and go well together and know in advance who will win. In this way, they destroy the simple people who trust them. This exegesis fits well with that of the little foxes as forms of misuse of language, because that is the exact weapon of bad advocates.

This pattern of exegesis was used not only in the study of the Bible but also in other text types, such as bestiaries and encyclopaedias, as will become clear in the next chapter. This implies that exegetical and 'biological' scholarship is partly interchangeable. So, when Hrabanus Maurus, the Archbishop of Mainz in the first half of the eighth century, wrote in his *De universo* (an encyclopaedia about the whole creation) about foxes he gave not only material information but also listed the possible allegorical meanings of foxes. His text shows that for medieval authors the individual Bible passages about the fox are all elements of the same coherent message. Thus, this part of his text can serve as summary of this section:

> Vulpes enim mystice diabolum dolosum, vel haereticum callidum, sive peccatorem hominem significat. Unde de Herode Dominus ait in Evangelio: Ite, dicite vulpi illi. Et alibi: Vulpes, inquit, foveas habeant: et volucres

coeli nidos; in vulpibus haereticos, et in volucribus coeli
malignos spiritus exprimens, qui in pectoribus humanis
sibi latibula quaerunt, ubi suggestiones suas perversas
interserant, et voluntates suas pessimas expleant. Item
vulpes diabolus vel daemones, ut in psalmo: Tradentur in
manus gladii, partes vulpium erunt. Et in Ieremia: Propter
montem Sion quia disperiit vulpes ambulaverunt in eo.
Vulpes, haeretici in Canticis canticorum: Capite nobis vulpes pusillas exterminantes vineas, id est plebes fidelium.[10]

The fox means in the spiritual sense the sly Devil, the
insidious heretic or the sinful man, hence the Lord said
about Herod in the Gospel: Go and tell that fox. And in
another place: Foxes, it is said, have holes and the birds
of the heaven have nests; the foxes signify the heretics
and the birds of the heaven evil spirits, who seek a resi-
dence in the human interior, where they introduce their
perverse suggestions and which they fill with their worst
wishes. The fox also signifies the Devil or demons, as in
the psalm: They shall fall by the sword: they shall be a
portion for foxes. And in Jeremiah: Because of the moun-
tain of Zion, which is desolate, the foxes walk upon it. The
foxes signify the heretics in the Song of Solomon: Take us
the foxes, the little foxes, that spoil the vines, that means
the faithful.

HAGIOGRAPHY

Hagiography is not an important genre for the study of the
medieval image of the fox because we find only a few foxes
in saints' lives, but these cases form an interesting addition
to the other material presented here. An important literary

topos in hagiography is the taming of a wild animal such as a bear, a wolf or a lion by a saint. Thus, a mortal danger is averted by his supernatural powers, which is a sign of God's grace. The meetings of a saint with a fox have a completely different character. They do not relate to lethal danger but to the handling of mischief.[11]

The Irish Columbanus founded the monastery of Bobbio in Italy. During his stay grapes were stolen from the vineyard. A monk discovered that a fox was the thief and forbade it to take any more grapes. However, the animal was 'accustomed to live by theft' and ignored the order. While eating the forbidden grapes, it died. St Moling had a pet fox that normally took its food from the saint's hands. Once, however, it ate a hen that belonged to another monk. Luckily the hen came back to life by a miracle. St Kieran was often visited by a fox that then carried his psalter. Once the nature of the fox took over and it damaged the leather bands around the psalter by gnawing on them. Hence, the saint's companions hunted the fox, but the saint sheltered the animal under his cowl and forgave it.

The most elaborate anecdote comes from the Life of St Brigid (after St Patrick the most important saint from Ireland). In St Brigid's time the king of Leinster kept a fox as a pet. It was able to do many tricks that the king enjoyed watching. A peasant, who came to the court, thought it was a wild fox and killed it. The king threatened to kill the peasant and sell his wife and sons into slavery unless he was able to produce a replacement. St Brigid was on her way to the court of Leinster and met a wild fox. He sought shelter under her cloak and went with her to the court. There he showed that he could do all the tricks and had all the skills

of the dead fox, so the king had to allow the peasant to go home unscathed. Soon after the release of the man and the departure of St Brigid, however, the wild nature of the fox took over and it escaped.

One could suppose that these anecdotes have only local importance and that their influence is restricted to Ireland. Bobbio, however, lies in Italy and the story of St Brigid became widespread. Her life was summarised by Vincent of Beauvais in his *Speculum historiale*, which during the Middle Ages was the most widespread and one of the most popular histories of the world. Vincent mentions the anecdote about the king of Leinster's fox, meaning that this anecdote was available in Latin in many places on the continent (we still have approximately 300 manuscripts left).

It would be incorrect to characterise the behaviour of these foxes simply as 'wrong'. The fox in Bobbio ignored an order and was punished immediately. The other foxes, however, seem to behave quite well normally but at certain moments relapse into their original wild nature. It seems as though the authors of these saints' lives simply could not imagine a fox that would be completely tame or behave correctly in all circumstances. This viewpoint fits the depictions and reports of vulpine obstinacy that we find in other medieval testimonies.

A remarkable aspect of these stories is that they show that in an Irish context a fox could be a tame animal, a pet. This is not a normal situation: the peasant thinks automatically that the fox he meets is wild. However, it is mentioned more than once, so it must not have been too extraordinary. I have not found any indication for comparable situations in other parts of Europe.

RELIGIOUS ROLES

There are many references and allusions to the fox assuming religious roles in medieval sources. He has been hermit, pilgrim, monk, friar, confessor, preacher, bishop, archbishop, cardinal and pope. However, the two most important roles are those of a preacher and a pilgrim. The fox as a preacher is found mostly in images, the fox as a pilgrim is found more often in stories.

The theme of the fox as a preacher has already been introduced as a proverb and as an image. When we consider the images of the preaching fox, we see three patterns emerge.[12] There are singular images of a fox preaching to birds, sometimes geese, sometimes a mixed flock with geese, cocks and chickens. The choice of these birds is not a coincidence. Geese are often a symbol of stupidity and cocks are often seen as vain and pompous. Stupid and vain people are easy to trick and, moreover, it is also easy to suggest that the victims are at least partly responsible for their own fate.

Some images of a fox preaching to geese are combined with an image of geese hanging the fox (Figures 3a and b). The trickster is tricked by his intended victims. And some images of a fox preaching to a flock are combined with an image of a farmer's wife, always with a distaff, who pursues the fox to retrieve her stolen bird (Figure 7). There are discrepancies between the images and the stories. It has already been remarked that we have no stories of a fox-preacher hanged by his flock afterwards. If such a story has existed, it was spread only orally and never added to the written record. We do, however, have stories of a fox running away with a stolen bird and pursued by a farmer's wife and her helpers, but in these stories the stolen bird is always

Figure 7. *Fox-bishop preaching to birds, and woman with distaff pursues a fleeing fox with goose. Smithfield decretals* (British Library, Roy. 10 E IV), *fol. 49v (illustrations ca. 1340).* © British Library.

a cock and never a goose, and the fox succeeds in grabbing his prey not by preaching but by playing on the vanity of his victim (see p. 92). Only in *Renart le Contrefait*, a late story (1319–42), does a fox succeeds in grabbing a cock by preaching to him.[13] In this tale, when Renart meets Chantecler the cock, Chantecler does not trust him. However, Renart assures him that his intentions are good and Christian because he is converted and that he wants to preach to Chantecler because the Lord ordered him to preach the Gospel. Renart had promised Chantecler's father to care for his children and he is very good at preaching. Less than three days ago Renart had preached for a whole day. 'Many a tear was shed there, and many a prayer recited … Many a nun slept and snored because of the good sermon they heard. Many a worthy man slept too. He who knows how to deliver a sermon makes men sleep, for those who sleep the best will come nearest to God.' Chantecler asks why Renart was converted. The fox answers that this had happened since he was able to hear the music of Paradise and the groans of Hell. The cock wants to share this experience. Renart decides to let Chantecler hear first the groans of Hell. However, he should not see or hear two things at the same moment, so he should look with one eye to the ground and one eye closed. The cock obeys and is grabbed by the fox who runs off with his prey.

The theme of the preaching fox – in both image and text – appears only from the thirteenth century onwards. This is probably no coincidence, it was during that century that the Franciscan and the Dominican orders were founded and preaching was the main task for both orders. As the Fourth Council of the Lateran (1215) had established more religious obligations for laypeople, it was inevitable that those laypeople would have more frequent contact with clerics and their preaching. The negative feelings that this might provoke could provide the background for the 'new' images of the fox-preacher and the variant of the fox-preacher in the tale of the capture of Chantecler by the fox.

The potential link between preacher and fox is also discernible in other stories besides *Renart le Contrefait*. In *Le Couronnement de Renart* (*c*.1260) Renart decides to become not only a Franciscan monk but also a Dominican. He does this to help both orders gain power at court, and they need Renart for that because as poor people they can strive for power only by guile and dirty tricks. Disguised as a cleric, Renart takes part in a plot to end the reign of King Noble. The plot succeeds, the king dies and Renart succeeds him. In the tale of *Renart le Nouvel* (last quarter of the thirteenth century) the Dominicans and the Franciscans both want to become rich without violating their rules. Hence, they

ask Renart to become their head. He refuses but gives the Dominicans his son Renardel and the Franciscans his son Roussel as their leader. In neither story does preaching play a prominent role but the content is related to the images of the fox-preacher because the preaching orders are presented as deceivers and as profiteers from others' trust through the use of ruses and lies.

The fox is used as an image of both false and ordinary friars. He can also represent the higher ranks of the ecclesiastical hierarchy. In some images of the fox-preacher, for instance, the fox has a mitre and a crosier, the symbols of a bishop (cf. Figure 7). And in *Le Couronnement de Renart*, Renart becomes not only a king but also a cardinal. In Rome he teaches the other cardinals his tricks and ever since they all behave like him. Perhaps the most interesting source in this context is the contemporary description in an anonymous metrical chronicle of the Pentecostal feast that Philippe le Bel, the king of France, organised in Paris in 1313.[14] As part of this enormous feast, *tableaux vivants* were driven through the city on carts. There were many types of tableau, often with religious themes, but there were also several featuring the fox. In one, he was seen reading an epistle and the gospel and another was characterised as showing his whole life, including how he devoured chickens and hens and that he was visible as bishop, pope and archbishop.[15] Modern scholars have different opinions on what exactly happened in the streets of Paris in 1313, but it is clear that the fox was presented to the spectators as representing the whole ecclesiastical hierarchy, right up to the highest offices. The underlying message must have been something like this: there are deceivers of laity in every rank of the Church. The fact that this message was spread via tableaux seen by the whole town implies that the fox as a figure for falsehood was familiar throughout society.

Let us now turn to the fox as a pilgrim. This role is found more often in texts than in images.[16] The oldest text in which the fox goes on a pilgrimage is *Ysengrimus* (1148–9).[17] In this early beast epic, Bertiliana the roe goes on a pilgrimage to see the relics of the saints. She is joined by Reinardus, the fox, and six other animals. The company stays for the night in a hospice and is joined there by the wolf Ysengrimus. They fear him but succeed in making the wolf so afraid that he wants to leave. As he leaves, he is mistreated by the pilgrims. Ysengrimus comes back with some relatives to take revenge and the pilgrims seek refuge on the roof. When the ass tries to climb up to the roof, he topples accidentally backwards onto two wolves. Reinardus praises this loudly as a fearless attack and the other wolves flee in terror. Later, two pilgrims, the cock and the goose, fear the cunning of the fox and decide to leave the group. As Reinardus is more interested in them as stuffing for his stomach than in religious merit as a pilgrim, he follows them and the pilgrimage plays no further role in the *Ysengrimus*. In this text the pilgrimage is not a central theme but one example among many of the conflicts between Reinardus and Ysengrimus.

This pilgrimage anecdote was retold as a separate tale in branch 8 of the *Roman de Renart*.[18] This story tells that on a Friday morning Renart lamented his sins and went to a hermit to confess. The hermit says that the sins are so serious that Renart must go to Rome to confess to the pope himself. En route, he gathers two companions: Belin the ram, who fears that his master will slaughter him; and Bernard the ass, who is weary of continually having to bear burdens. They stay the night in the house of the wolf Primaut, but when the wolf and his wife Hersent come back, the pilgrims trap Primaut in the doorway and kill him. Hersent goes away and collects more than 100 other wolves to take revenge. They follow the fleeing pilgrims who seek safety up a tree. The wolves, who lose the trail under the tree, rest there. Belin and Bernard can hold on no longer and fall out of the tree. Bernard squashes four wolves, Belin kills two more. Renart applauds this loudly as a fearless attack and the wolves fly in fright. After this experience, the pilgrims realise that going on pilgrimage is far more dangerous than they had thought and that the situation at home was preferable. 'At that, they all shouted "Onward! Onward!" and made their way back!'[19] The story's first aim is of course to amuse, but it shows also that it is wise to think first before you begin. Renart plays his traditional role; he makes the best of an unexpected development and it is clear that the repentance of his sins is not very sincere. He says to himself: 'There's many a worthy man in this world who has never been to Rome, whereas some other has returned from seven pilgrimages worse than he was before.' Good deeds can also be done at home.

The idea that the fox should go to Rome to seek forgiveness for his sins is taken up in the two Dutch Reynaert stories, *Van den vos Reynaerde* and *Reynaerts historie* (see pp. 96–100). They tell that Reynaert came to court and was sentenced to be hanged. The fox asks to be allowed to give a public confession before he dies, during which he claims that he saved the king's life. He had done so by stealing a treasure that Reynaert's father wanted to use to finance a revolt and the replacement of King Nobel by Bruun the bear. The king and queen are very interested in that treasure, so in exchange for a pardon Reynaert promises the king his treasure and describes the place where it is hidden. Not knowing the treasure's hiding place, the king demands Reynaert accompany him there, but Reynaert claims that this is, alas, impossible. He is excommunicated and must go to Rome to obtain absolution from the pope and afterwards he must travel to the Holy Land in expiation of his sins. He asks for help for this pilgrimage and gets a scrip made from a piece of skin of Bruun the bear and four shoes that cost Ysegrim and Hersint, his wife, the skin of two paws apiece. Through the lie about the treasure he saves his life, and through the lie about the necessity of his pilgrimage he avoids accompanying the king to the hiding place of the non-existent treasure.

Pilgrimage is of vital importance in this story because it is the final element in the fox's ruse to save his life and to escape the king. The narrator gives his audience many signs that Reynaert is a liar and a false pilgrim. Before he relates the fox's confession, he announces that Reynaert will lie blatantly. At the moment when Reynaert is ready to leave the court, the narrator points out that Reynaert is false and ridiculous:

> Mi dinct ende ic wane des,
> dat niement so onspellic es
> tusschen Pollanen ende Scouden,
> die hem van lachene hadde onthouden

> dor rauwe die hem mochte ghescien,
> hadde hi Reynaerde doe ghesien!
> Hoe wonderlic hi henenghinc
> ende hoe ghemackelic dat hem hinc
> scaerpe ende palster omme den hals
> ende die scoen als ende als
> die hi droech an zine been
> ghebonden, sodat hi sceen
> een peelgrijn licht ghenouch![20]

> I am convinced that / there is no one so downhearted / between Poland and Schouwen / because of a disaster that had befallen him, / or he would have laughed / on seeing Reynaert then! / How amazing his departure was / and how naturally did / the scrip and staff hang around his neck / and did he wear all the shoes / that he had tied around his legs, / so that he might quite easily / have been taken for a pilgrim!

The image of Reynaert creates hilarity and contains a contradiction: the wearing of shoes makes him human, but that he has four shoes stresses his animal nature (cf. Figure 8). The last two lines stress a further important point, that the fox may be easily taken for a pilgrim implies that he is not one. Perhaps the narrator goes even further in warning against the falsity of Reynaert because at the beginning of his story Reynaert is twice presented as a hermit, a role that is the opposite of a pilgrim because a hermit stays in one place and a pilgrim travels. In the Dutch Reynaert tradition, Reynaert is presented as a resourceful and highly skilled liar, whichever religious role he plays.

Figure 8. *Reynard receives his pilgrim attributes and takes leave of the king.* Wynkyn de Worde *woodcut (c.1495) for the* History of Reynard the Fox, *the English adaptation of* Reynaerts historie.

CONCLUSION

In all these religious contexts the fox is linked with deceit, fraud and deception, but also with cunning and ingenuity. In most he is judged negatively. The fox is even linked to the Devil in many cases of Bible exegesis. The mood is less severe in other contexts; in hagiographies and other stories his tricks cause no irreparable damage and one can laugh with him.

CHAPTER 2

THE FOX AND MEDIEVAL SCHOLARSHIP

MODERN BIOLOGY, like all modern sciences, is based on observation and experiment. Medieval biological scholarship, like all medieval scholarship, is based firmly on the study of books, more precisely on the study of those texts that are seen as the authorities for that specific field of knowledge. The hunting manuals that will be presented here form an exception to this rule because the material that they discuss is in large part based on existing practical knowledge and the cumulative experience of generations of hunters. However, many later hunting manuals are translations or base themselves on older sources, so even in this very practical genre we may discern the 'bookish' character of medieval scholarship.

Another general remark that must be made is that in the Middle Ages scholarship was rarely seen as an aim in itself. The pinnacle of intellectual life was theology and other branches of scholarship were considered her 'handmaidens'. More generally, it can be observed that all types of intellectual knowledge were also used for religious aims: to instruct people in the true doctrine and the just way of life and to exhort them to believe the first and to follow the second. This is evident in bestiaries and encyclopaedias,

the first two scholarly genres to be presented here, but this tendency may also be found in hunting manuals, as will become clear.

BESTIARIES

Bestiaries are medieval didactic texts that use animals and animal lore to instruct the recipients in Christian spiritual, especially moral, ideas.[1] The twelfth century was the heyday of the Latin bestiaries but we find Latin bestiaries throughout the whole of the Middle Ages, and vernacular ones from the twelfth century onwards. The tradition, however, begins in the early Christian era. In the second or third century a Greek text, the *Physiologus*, was written in Alexandria, then a very important centre of learning. There are variant versions of the *Physiologus*, but they all contain separate chapters about natural phenomena: not only animals, but also birds, stones and creatures like centaurs and sirens. In these chapters, the scholarly knowledge about a thing is combined with moral teaching, based on an allegorical interpretation, comparable to the allegorical interpretations of things from the Bible (see pp. 26–7). The two parts of a chapter are called the 'nature' and the 'allegory'.

The *Physiologus* was translated fairly quickly into Latin and developed into several versions. In the eleventh century, the *Physiologus* material was enriched by additions from the *Etymologiae* of Isidore of Seville (see pp. 59–60) and other texts about the natural world.[2] These enriched texts form the bestiary tradition proper. Specialists divide the tradition into groups, but that division need not concern us here because the chapters about the fox are remarkably stable throughout the whole tradition from the Greek *Physiologus* to the vernacular versions of the later Middle Ages.[3] As a representative of the whole tradition I cite here the chapter on the fox in the so-called 'second-family bestiary':

Vulpis dicitur quasi volupis. Est enim volobilis pedibus et numquam recto itinere, sed tortuosis anfractibus currit. Est etiam fraudulentium animal et ingeniosum. Cum esurit et non invenit quod manducet, involuit se in rubea terra, ut appartet quasi cruentata, et proicit se in terram, retinetque flatum suum ita ut penitus non spiret. Aves vero videntes eam non flantem et quasi cruentatam, linguamque eius foris erectam, putant eam esse mortuam, et descendunt sessum super eam. Illa autem sic rapit eas et devorat.

Istius eiusdemque figuram Diabolus possidet. Omnibus enim viventibus secundum carnem fingit se esse mortuum, quoadusque inter guttur suum habeat et puniat. Spiritualibus tamen viris in fide verum mortuus est et ad nihilum redactus. Qui autem volunt exercere opera eius moriuntur, dicente apostolo, Sciatis hoc quia si secundum carmen vixeritis, moriemini. Si autem spiritu facta carnis mortificaveritis, vivetis (Romans 8:13). Et David, Intrabun in inferiora terrae: tradentur in manus gladii, partes vulpium erunt (Psalm 62:10–11).[4]

He is called fox (*vulpis*), as it were, sensual (*volupis*). Now, he has speedy feet and never runs in a straight line, but in circuitous twists. He is a deceitful and crafty animal. When he is hungry and cannot find something to eat, he rolls in red soil so that he appears to be bloodied, and lies down on the ground, and hold his breath so that he

does not breathe at all. Now, the birds seeing the fox not breathing and as though bloodied, and his tongue hanging out, think that he is dead, and fly down to sit upon him. But it is by this means that he seizes and eats them.

And the Devil takes that animal's form. To all those living by the flesh he pretends that he is dead, until he has them in his maw and punishes them. Yet to spiritual men in faith he is truly dead and reduced to nothing. Those, however, who want to carry out his work die, as the apostle says, That you may know this because *if you live according to the flesh, you shall die: but if by the* Spirit *you mortify the deeds of the flesh, you shall live.* And David says, They *shall go into the lower parts of the earth: they shall be delivered into the hands of the sword, they shall be the portion of foxes.*

The opening of this chapter is taken from the *Etymologiae* (see pp. 59–60). The rest of the 'nature' is the description of a ruse (cf. Figures 6 and 11). This is also described in the *Etymologiae*, but it stems from the *Physiologus*. The ruse perhaps seems farfetched, but in 1961 a fox was filmed in the Caucasus as it feigned death to catch a crow,[5] so this description does relate to the actual behaviour of foxes. In the 'allegory' the fox is interpreted as the Devil. Just as the fox deceived the birds and lured them with his seemingly dead flesh, so the Devil deceives humans by luring them with worldly goods. But when you strive for the heavenly reward, you have nothing to fear from him. This interpretation is supported by two quotations from the Bible. The first is linked to the flesh that the fox uses as a lure. The second is seen as an 'announcement' of what happens in the 'nature' part.

This is essentially what all Latin bestiaries write about the fox. Where there are differences, they concern the level of explanation (more or less extensive) and the Bible quotations that are added. As the fox may be interpreted as the Devil in all the quotations, variation is easily possible. In some vernacular bestiaries, we find greater differences, mainly because of a tendency to explain more fully The *Bestiaire* of Pierre de Beauvais (early thirteenth century), for instance, states that the birds signify those people who want to do the works of the Devil. And what are those works? Fornication, homicide, theft and false testimony.[6] And the *Bestiaire divin* of Guillaume le Clerc de Normandie (1210–11) opens with a reference to what the public already knows: You have heard enough about the ways Renart used to steal the chickens of Constant de Noues (a rich farmer in the *Roman de Renart*), says Guillaume. He wants to devour hens and capons in all seasons. He continually lives on pillage, theft and deception, because he is a traitor and of a despicable race.[7] We see here that an author assumes his public knows tales about Reynard the fox and he merges the images of Reynard and the bestiary fox. Both deceive, both are malicious and bad.

The bestiary anecdote about the fox feigning death became extremely popular. Via the *Etymologiae* it became part of the encyclopaedic tradition, and many other texts mention this ruse, for instance, *Les livres du roy Modus et de la royne Ratio*, a hunting manual that will be discussed further on in this chapter (see pp. 66–76). The ruse was also told as a fable and was used in stories about Reynard.[8] In the branch of the *Roman de Renart* that told the story of Renart's funeral (XVII), the fox falls into a swoon that is so deep that the other animals think he is dead. He is laid in a grave but

at the moment the bear begins to shovel earth into the grave Renart awakens, jumps out of the grave, grabs Chantecler the cock and runs away. Later in the same branch, a duel is described between Chantecler and Renart. Chantecler does so well that Renart feigns death to prevent himself from actually being killed. The animals leave his 'dead body' in a ditch, where he lies on his back with open jaws. Rohart the rook wants to eat of this 'corpse', but Renart springs back to life and snaps off one of Rohart's thighs.[9] So here we see two separate references to the bestiary ruse in one story, which is understandable because this story plays continually, and in many ways, with the themes of death and funeral.

The anecdote is also used in *Reynaerts historie* (see pp. 98–100),[10] where it is told twice, the first time by Corbout the rook. He says that he and his wife Scerpenebbe saw Reynaert's 'dead body' and flew down to the 'corpse' to see whether they could help (how nice of these carrion birds), but Reynaert then grabbed his wife and killed her. The second time the story is told by Reynaert himself. He explains Scerpenebbe's death by saying that she ate too much carrion and that the maggots it contained split her belly, thus playing with the ruse by presenting an extravagant result of the feeding habits of a carrion crow. And besides, how would he have been able to catch her? After all, Scerpenebbe could fly and he could not, so Corbout's story must be a lie. Here the fox ignores the fact that Corbout's story explains precisely how the fox could grab his wife, but because the rook is afraid of the fox, he does not protest but quietly leaves the court. So here the bestiary ruse is used to show how egotistical behaviour can be presented as altruistic and how a complaint can be simply refuted by presenting another version of the events under discussion.

Finally, a few remarks on Richard de Fournival's *Bestiaire d'amour*.[11] Richard de Fournival (1201–60) was chancellor of Notre-Dame, the cathedral of Amiens. His *Bestiaire d'amour* uses the traditional bestiary knowledge in a new way: to ask a lady for her love. He has tried everything to win that love but nothing has worked. Now he sends his lady this work as a last effort. He calls it his *arriere ban*, that part of an army that is kept in reserve for the decisive moment in a battle. It is unclear whether the text is truly serious. It contains many intellectual jokes, and many passages appear mocking or derisive and are not very flattering to women. However, the passage about the fox is completely clear:

> Et teus dist qu'il se meurt d'amours, qu'il n'en sent ne mal ne dolour, et en dechoivent la bone gent ausi com li gorpiex fait les piies. Car li gorpiex est de tele nature que quant il a faim et il ne trove ke mangier, il se touelle en la boe de rouge terre, et se couche geule baee la langue fors, aussi com s'il fust mors sanglens. Et lors viennent les piies ki mort le quident, si li voellent manguer le langue. Et il gete les dens, si les prent par les testes et les deveure.[12]

> A man will say he is dying of love when he feels no pain or hurt, and these deceive good folk just as the fox deceives the magpies. For the fox is of such a nature that when it is hungry and finds nothing to eat, it will roll in the mud of red earth and will lie down with its jaws hanging open and its tongue out, as if it had bled to death. Then come the magpies, thinking it dead, and they try to eat the tongue. And the fox bares its teeth, seizes them by the head, and devours them.

Richard writes this almost at the end of his text. He states that there are many lovers who only pretend to be in love to reach their goal by trickery, just as the fox did by pretending to be dead. In his presentation of the ruse Richard introduces a variation. Normally the birds want to eat the flesh of the fox. Here, they want to eat the tongue. It is not made explicit, but I believe that Richard introduces this variation because the false lovers deceive their girlfriends by talking and the tongue is the instrument of speech. Richard continues by saying that his lady will perhaps think that he is such a false lover. But there are many reasons to join the army. (Here Richard returns to the military metaphor with which he started.) Vultures follow armies because they want to eat carrion. Men who want only to profit from ladies behave in the same way. Yet there are also people in armies who are there to serve their lord. Such is the case with Richard. He would like to show his fidelity to his lady, but that is impossible as long as she refuses him. Hence, he ends by asking for mercy, a traditional request of rejected lovers.

Although the *Bestiaire d'amour* was controversial (using religious material to manipulate worldly love) and not easy to interpret, it was clearly popular. However, because of its at times very misogynistic content, it could also be rejected, especially by women, as is shown by a second text that is added in some manuscripts to the *Bestiaire d'amour*. It is called the *Réponse de la dame*. It is anonymous and there is no indication that it was also written by Richard, but it is clearly related to his *Bestiaire*, because it has the same structure and refutes all his arguments. The passage in the *Réponse* about the fox is most remarkable.

Both the *Bestiaire d'amour* and the *Réponse* were written in the time that the traditional word for fox, *goupil*, was slowly replaced by a new noun, *renard*, based on the proper name Renart, used in the popular fox stories. According to tradition, Richard had named the fox goupil (*gorpiex*). The lady, however, uses *renard* and equates the fox with the author. After all, there is a certain likeness between the names 'Richard' and 'Renart':

> Ahi Renart, con vous avés le langue traite hors sans raison; et sans faille sans aucune raison, n'est che pas? Car je cuit bien que s'il n'eüst fain, ja ne se meteroit ou point, qu'il se met, ensi que jou ai entendu.[13]

> Ah, Reynard, how far out your tongue is hanging! For no reason, of course, I suppose! I am sure that if Reynard were not hungry, his tongue would never hang out in the way I heard.

Here the wickedness and the deceiving manners of the fox are projected onto the author and lover, Richard, and the lady rejects the words of his *Bestiaire d'amour* as false and his love as feigned, especially by stating that his tongue is hanging out of his mouth not by necessity but as a ruse for gain. We can ignore the question of the fairness of the lady's rejection. Both Richard's and the lady's interpretation of the fox are identical and completely in line with the traditional interpretation of the fox in other bestiaries. That they use this interpretation in different ways is for us less important than the insight into how stable the meaning of the bestiary fox is in all types of text where it is found.

ENCYCLOPAEDIAS

Medieval scholars did not use the term 'encyclopaedia'.[14] This was attributed by modern researchers to those medieval texts that aim to present all the available knowledge about the world, or about a part of it or a specific field of scholarship. Those texts that collect all the available knowledge about creatures are a very useful source for the modern scholar who wants to study a specific animal. This type of medieval encyclopaedia differs from bestiaries because in bestiaries the allegorical interpretation is always added to the biological information. Encyclopaedias, however, concentrate in the first instance on the scholarly information, and they contain, certainly from the thirteenth century onwards, much more varied information than the bestiaries. The allegorical meaning, however, was mostly omitted. But we will see that encyclopaedic knowledge was nevertheless also used to produce allegorical interpretations.

To write about the fox in medieval encyclopaedias I have consulted several Latin texts: Isidore of Seville, *Etymologiae* (early seventh century), Hrabanus Maurus, *De universo* (first half of the nineth century), Alexander Neckam, *De naturis rerum* (c.1190), Thomas of Cantimpré, *De natura rerum* (between 1225 and 1244), Bartholomaeus Anglicus, *De proprietatibus rerum* (mid-thirteenth century), Vincent of Beauvais, *Speculum naturale* (mid-thirteenth century) and Albertus Magnus, *De animalibus* (mid-thirteenth century).[15] The *Etymologiae* is the oldest and most influential medieval encyclopaedic text and its content is reproduced by almost all later encyclopaedias. The texts of Hrabanus Maurus and Alexander Neckam are chosen because they represent the 'middle period' and because they contain some allegorical interpretations. In the thirteenth century, scholarship changed markedly because many Aristotelian texts became available via Latin translations of Arabic translations of and commentaries on the original Greek texts. This influx changed the approaches of scholars and they gained access to new information. The main transmitter of Aristotelian biology was Michael Scot's Latin translation, *Historia animalium* (early thirteenth century). We find this Aristotelian influence in all thirteenth century encyclopaedias, most strongly in Albertus' *De animalibus*. Regarding the information about the fox, however, the influence of Aristotle was minor.[16]

Thomas of Cantimpré's text was translated and adapted into Dutch by Jacob van Maerlant (*c*.1270) and into German by Konrad von Megenberg (*c*.1350). *De proprietatibus rerum* was translated into French by Jean Corbechon (1372), into English by John Trevisa (1397), and later Dutch (before 1485), Occitan, Italian and Spanish. I leave these vernacular versions out, and likewise original vernacular encyclopaedias such as Brunetto Latini's *Livre du Trésor* (1263–4), because they contain in principle the same information that the Latin encyclopaedias provide. The texts I discuss form a reliable representation of the knowledge a medieval scholar could glean about foxes, in whatever language he found it.

Isidore of Seville is brief on the fox. He writes:

Vulpes dicta, quasi volupes. Est enim volubilis pedibus, et numquam rectis itineribus, sed tortuosis anfractibus currit, fraudulentum animal insidiisque decipiens. Nam dum non habuerit escam, fingit mortem, sique descentes quasi ad cadaver aves rapit et devorat.[17]

> Foxes (*vulpes*) are so named as if the word were *volupes*, for
> they are 'shifty on their feet' (*volubilis* and *pes*) and never
> follow a straight path but hurry along tortuous twistings.
> It is a deceitful animal, tricking others with its guile, for
> whenever it has no food it pretends to be dead, and so it
> snatches and devours the birds that descend to its appar-
> ent corpse.

As usual, Isidore starts with the etymology of the word
vulpes. (This principle gives his work its title.) Modern etymology explains the form of a word by describing its historical development. Medieval etymology assumes that
the structure of the material world and the structure of
language are analogous because they were both created
by God. This assumption leads to the idea that the form of
words refers to characteristic properties of the things that
they indicate. In this case, *vulpes* is related to *volubilis* (shifting, winding) and *pes* (feet). In this way the form of the word
vulpes indicates that foxes never walk straight but always
in a winding way. Then Isidore characterises the fox as a
deceitful animal, full of tricks. And, lastly, he mentions the
ruse from the P*hysiologus* that illustrates this fraudulence. All
three elements were maintained throughout the whole of
the encyclopaedic tradition.

That the fox never walks in a straight line, is often mentioned, even when the etymology is not given. Mostly this
is just stated, but Thomas of Cantimpré gives a 'psychological' explanation by stating that he does this because he
does not want to be noticed by the hunters. Bartholomeus
Anglicus gives a 'biological' explanation. He says that the
fox always limps because his right feet are shorter than his

left feet. Whatever the explanation, the winding ways of the fox are always interpreted as a sign of his deviousness.

The fox's craftiness and cunning are mostly indicated by the use of the Latin adjectives *fraudulosus* (deceitful) and *dolosus* (sly). Less often we find *fallax* (deceptive), *astutus* (crafty), *ingeniosus* (clever) and *subdolus* (sneaky). They all indicate that he is shrewd and guileful. Alexander Neckam even states that the fox's cleverness can at times deceive humans (p. 204). Ingenuity and slyness are seen as his most important characteristics and they are regularly illustrated with examples.

The longest passage exemplifying the cleverness of the fox can be found in the *Speculum naturale*, where Vincent dedicates a whole chapter (book 19, cap. 122) to this topic. He starts, of course, with the fox feigning death from the bestiary tradition and then adds ruses such as that a fox can bark like a dog and sometimes he escapes by running into a pack of dogs while barking loudly. The dogs become confused by this barking and the fox slips away. Alternatively, a hunted fox flees towards a herd of goats and jumps on the back of one of them. This startled goat then runs away, followed by the whole herd. Then the hunter calls back his hounds to prevent more havoc and the fox escapes. When the fox is caught in a trap, he is willing to bite off a part of his paw to escape, and when he sees no other remedy he feigns death in the hope that an opportunity to escape will arise when he is taken up as a corpse. The fox is equally crafty with other animals; for example, he takes over the sett of a badger by soiling it (more on this later). Similarly, foxes try to play with hares and catch a distracted one, but most hares refuse to play because they do not trust foxes.

A fox takes circuitous routes to hide his tracks and when he must travel across frozen water, he first lays his ear on the ice. If he still can hear the water, he does not trust the ice and goes back.

Two ruses not mentioned in this chapter are also worthy of note. Alexander Neckam writes that once a fox was chased by a hunter and his dogs. In headlong flight he entered a house and came to a room where many pelts lay on the ground. Lying between them, he kept completely still so that the hunter did not notice him at first. It was only because the dogs pertinently refused to leave the room that the fox was discovered in the end (p. 204). Albertus Magnus writes about how a fox infested with fleas takes a stick in its mouth and then slowly walks backwards into the water. The fleas all flee to his head for fear of the water. If the fox then ducks his head under the water, the fleas jump on the stick. The fox spits out the stick and leaves the water without fleas (p. 1427, pars 147).

What has been discussed up to now is found throughout the encyclopaedic tradition and concerns mainly the 'mental' properties of foxes. In the thirteenth century texts (and partly already in Neckam) we find more information. A new 'mental' element is added: foxes are *vorax et gulosum* (gluttonous and cruel). This is the reason that the fox cubs are born blind, as Bartholomaeus Anglicus states, for if they were fully formed they would kill their mother when she suckled them. Alexander Neckam says that the young wound their mother internally with their claws because of their savage nature. However, the additional information in the thirteenth-century texts regards mainly the bodily properties of the fox. Attention is paid to his medical uses (see p. 6) and to three elements in particular: the fox's stench, his burrow and his tail.

It is sometimes stated in general terms that a fox stinks from his mouth and from his backside. The places where he stays for any length of time become barren and spoiled. This stench makes it unpleasant to be near him and that is how the fox uses his bodily odour as a weapon. In the first place, the stench gets him a burrow. Since biblical times it has been a literary topos that foxes have holes, but the thirteenth-century encyclopaedias explain how they obtain them. A fox does not create a hole or burrow himself but takes it from the badger. He waits until the badger leaves his sett to obtain food. He then enters the sett and soils it with his excrement. When the badger returns, he abhors the terrible stench and because he is a very clean animal he does not want to stay. He goes away and digs a new hole and the fox takes over the old one. Bartholomeus Anglicus links this behaviour to the deviousness of the fox and Thomas of Cantimpré sees it as an example of misuse of what another created with effort. Alexander Neckam links this behaviour of the fox to a specific form of theft: the usurpation of a domain. He adds that luckily this misdeed is often corrected when the true lord is restored and the usurper must go away and live in poor circumstances in a remote area (p. 207).

This element in the encyclopaedic knowledge is remarkable because it differs from the situation in stories. In the animal epic Grimbert the badger is a nephew of Reynard and his staunchest supporter. To my knowledge, this is the only significant difference between the two traditions. Bohdana Librová has suggested two possible explanations for this

difference.[18] The theft of the badger's sett by the fox was very often used in *exempla* (short stories to illustrate a moral point). When the inventors of the stories sought a loyal ally for the fox it was the badger that came to mind because he was already so often linked to the fox. The second explanation is based on observation of nature. Badger setts tend to be spacious and contain many compartments. Hence, we know now that badgers and foxes may live together in the same burrow without conflict.[19] The friendship of Reynard and Grimbert could be based on this ecological fact. Yet for me, both explanations are unconvincing. When two characters are frequently portrayed as enemies, it makes no sense to present them as friends. And I find it very strange to assume that the same direct observation of a biological situation would in the encyclopaedic tradition lead to a negative interpretation, and in literature to a positive one. Why this difference? I think it is better to accept that we do not have an answer to this riddle.

The last new element in the descriptions is the fox's tail, which is characterised by the encyclopaedias as big and bushy. In certain circumstances, he uses it as a weapon against dogs. Sometimes it is said that the fox forces his tail into the mouths of the chasing dogs. Many hairs stay behind in the mouths and between the teeth of the dogs. The dogs, disliking this, recoil for a moment, which is enough for the fox to escape. In other texts, it is written that the fox wets his tail with his own foul-smelling urine and chases the dogs away with the stench. Thus, we see that the fox's stench is linked both to his burrow and his tail. The thirteenth-century image of the fox is more elaborate than the older one, but just as coherent.

Until now I have only hinted at allegorical interpretations of the information that is given about the fox. As already said, this type of interpretation is rare in the encyclopaedic tradition proper, but that this material could be (and was) used for allegoresis becomes clear when we look at a non-encyclopaedic text, the *Reductorium morale* of Petrus Berchorius (or in French: Pierre Bersuire, *c*.1290–1362). Petrus Berchorius was a French Benedictine monk whose *Reductorium morale* was designed to assist preachers. Inside, they could, in principle, find the possible allegorical meanings of the whole of creation. The book follows the structure of *De proprietatibus rerum* closely and gives the same information, but in all cases is complemented by allegoresis. Here are a few examples:[20] that foxes never run in a straight line is linked to the behaviour of usurers, deceivers, evil and greedy people. In making their contracts and legal agreements they do not act correctly but tortuously (i.e., they are full of deceit and cunning, because their right foot – that is their intention – always limps as a result of falseness). This is because in their words and their deeds they always show one thing but aim at another. That the fox steals the badger's burrow is interpreted in two ways. In the first reading, the badger is Christ, the burrow is the human heart, and the fox is the Devil who befouls the heart with his stinking sins. In the second reading, the badger stands for good people, and the fox for bad people who envy what they see in the possession of others.[21] That the fox befouls his environment is also interpreted in two ways. The fox is an allegory for slanderers, lechers, hypocrites and heretics because they are rotten and reek of vice and sin. They ruin others with

their bad words and their bad example. The fox is also an allegory for the Devil because his bite (i.e., temptation) and his breath (i.e., suggestion) are poisoned. As he is depraved by malice and sin, he also corrupts others by letting them sin and stopping them from doing good works. The fox who fills the mouth of the chasing dogs with hairs from his tail stands for the rich and the usurers who present gifts to bad judges to obtain a favourable verdict. Or else the dogs represent preachers who dare not accuse the wicked because they fear their slander and aggression. A final example is the fox who wants to cross the ice but first lays his ear on it to hear how thick it is. The ice stands for worldly honour or prosperity, which is always fragile. When an office or an opportunity for worldly gain is offered to you, you should first check if you hear the sound of water – that is, a warning from the scriptures. If you do not hear it, you can accept the offer, but if you hear a warning it is better to remain inconspicuous or poor. Only this example gives a positive spin on vulpine behaviour.

These examples show the versatility and the general applicability of an allegorical interpretation of the world. They also show clearly that the fox is seen in a negative light and is almost always linked to deceit and corruption.

HUNTING MANUALS

Hunting played a very important role in medieval society.[22] All social classes hunted for various reasons, such as to remove danger or to obtain food, as training for war, as sport or for socialising. Most of the information we have about medieval hunting comes from extant hunting manuals.[23] These were written originally in Latin and later in many of the vernaculars. It is important to realise that these books were written in and for aristocratic circles. They do not describe all hunting techniques, nor do they express all possible attitudes towards hunting.

The aristocracy used mainly two types of hunting: falconry and venery. Falconry is hunting with birds of prey, venery is hunting with dogs, either on foot with hounds on leashes or on horseback with free-running dogs. Birds were never used to hunt foxes, so we must turn to treatises on venery to learn more. It seems as though the fox hunt was more popular in France and England than in other parts of Europe. Hence the information given here is based on three manuals, two from France and one from England.[24] The first is *Les livres du roy Modus et de la royne Ratio*, which is ascribed to Henri de Ferrières, an author about whom we know only his name. It was written between 1354 and 1377. The second is *Le livre de chasse* written between 1385 and 1387 by Gaston Phébus (i.e., Gaston III, Count of Foix), regarded as one of the best hunters of his day. His treatise has become very influential. The third is *The Master of Game*, an English adaptation of the *Livre de chasse* by Edward of Norwich, the second Duke of York. It was written between 1406 and 1413. The fact that two of the three authors are from the highest ranks of the nobility, indicates the importance of hunting for aristocratic circles. The information in these three manuals runs fairly parallel, although it is organised differently. They all describe the properties of foxes and give advice on how to hunt them.

There is some specific information in the manuals regarding the vixen. This is absent in other genres. The reason is probably that the other genres discuss the fox as

a species, but for a hunter, the different behaviours of the male and the female representatives of a species may be important. The vixen is in heat once a year and is pregnant for about the same duration as a she-wolf's pregnancy (this comparison with the she-wolf is found only in the hunting manuals). During her pregnancy she stays very close to her den to ensure that she is always able to hide at the smallest sign of danger. According to the hunting books, the vixen keeps her whelps underground, but deeper than the she-wolf does. Her bite can prove toxic, just like that of a wolf, although her life is a little shorter than that of a wolf. When in heat she lures the dog fox with a hoarse cry, just like that of a mad dog. She makes the same noise when she calls her whelps. The manuals characterise her as a false beast and more malicious than the she-wolf.

The manuals also include more general information: foxes live in great hedges or in extensive dens or burrows, often near villages or towns where they seek their prey. They eat vermin, carrion and worms, but their preferred food is fowl (cf. Figure 9). When they can, they eat hens, capons, ducks and young geese,[25] but also small wild birds, butterflies, grasshoppers, milk and butter. They also eat hares and coneys, which they catch not by running but by cunning tricks. These ideas about the eating habits of foxes correspond to what we find in other types of text. Encyclopaedias say that foxes prefer tame animals above wild ones and in literary texts, at least in Irish and German ones, foxes are presented as scavengers in descriptions of the aftermath of a battle or raid.[26] The fox is not strong and must therefore defend himself by cunning. He hides in holes or undergrowth and he shuns the open field because

Figure 9. *Foxes prefer to eat fowl. Here a fox has captured a duck* (*cf. 'queck'*). *Gorleston psalter* (British Library, Add. 49622), *fol. 190v (second decade of fourteenth century).* © British Library Board.

he dare not rely on his speed or strength. He stinks and when he is sorely pressed by hounds, he uses his excrement to make them shrink from him. This strategy works well. Quite a few dogs who do not hesitate to attack a boar or a wolf will not pursue a fox. The pelt of a dead fox is wonderfully warm and very suitable for mittens or lining garments, but will smell if not properly prepared. Fox grease and marrow are useful for strengthening sinews (which are used as binding material).

The most interesting way of hunting foxes is *par force de chiens* ('by strength of dogs'), the forerunner of modern fox

hunting (Figure 10).[27] In this type of hunt an area is closed off and the prey is driven by dogs in such a way that, in the end, the fox cannot escape. It is a quite elaborate action, as the following description shows.

> First seek out an isolated wood, then block all the fox-holes you can find. To do this job well you must look for the holes a day or two before you plan the hunt. These holes should be blocked when the moon is full, or nearly full, at about midnight. Block them with a small bundle of sticks pushed firmly into the opening and on top of that pile a mound of earth. On top of this mound place two pointed sticks in the form of a cross. The fox will never come near his hole when he sees the crossed sticks because he will think it is some trap or other set for him. When it is broad daylight on the day of the hunt, take your dogs and as many men as you can muster to the wood and have them surround it. Then let three or four of your best dogs loose. If they find the fox, let more dogs loose, then you will have a most enjoyable time as you watch the fox flee, then twist and turn, then stand still, then attack the dogs, then begin to flee again. He tries to leave the wood altogether and dashes out into the open, but the men who surround the wood shout and force him back. Then you release more dogs. If you follow this advice you will witness a fine battle and have a most enjoyable hunt. Usually the dogs tear him to pieces with their teeth.[28]

The dogs that are released during the hunt are brought beforehand to places where the fox will probably pass

Figure 10. Par force *fox hunt. Illustration in a copy of the* Livre de la chasse *by Gaston Phébus. New York, the Morgan Library and Museum, Ms M. 1044 (bequest of Clara S. Peck 1983), fol. 88v (c.1406–7).*

during his flight. If this happens, fresh dogs can take up the hunt. It is organised as a kind of relay race for the dogs and the hunters.

Sir Gawain and the Green Knight contains the description of such a fox hunt. The pattern of the hunt is very alike in both texts, but *Sir Gawain* evokes more strongly the joy that the hunt gives to the hunters. It also describes the end, which is touched on only lightly in the manuals. Sir Bertilak (the main hunter in *Sir Gawain*) wrenches the body of the fox from the hounds, lifts it and gives a halloo. All the hunters gather and together they sound a horn signal and shout a loud halloo in praise of the spirit of the fox, for – as the

hunting manuals state – the fox does not cry out when he dies but, as long as he lives, he defends himself with all his ability. The musical ending of the hunt is a sign of respect for the fox's attitude.[30]

The first three months of the year are the best time for fox hunting. This does not imply that foxes will not be hunted during the rest of the year, but the *par force* hunt described here, is restricted to January, February and March. This is the best time for three reasons: during this period the fox's fur is of the highest quality (so Sir Bertilak is not the only hunter saving the fox's pelt from the dogs); the trees are bare so it is easier to find the foxholes to block them and to see the fox fleeing through the woods; and, lastly, foxes eat salamanders and snakes during the summer, which can make the fox (more) poisonous, meaning that many dogs may then refuse to hunt them.

There are other methods for hunting foxes, some of which are indicated in the manuals. When a fox hides in a den, he can be dug out if the den is not in rocky ground, but a better method is to smoke him out: close all the entrances with one exception, facing the wind. Place burning embers previously sprinkled with sulphur as deep as possible in one of the blocked entrances. The poisonous smoke will drive the fox to the one remaining exit and once he is out he can be hunted by the dogs. Variations of this method were probably the usual ways of hunting foxes. We find indications of the use of traps, snares, nets and poisons to catch foxes and for the use of terriers or (sulphurous) smoke to drive them out of their dens.[31] In Germany artificial, moveable hedges were also used, which had openings with snares in them.[32] Nets and snares were not always effective, however, because foxes can cut them with their teeth, just as wolves do, only slower.

These methods were used mainly by the lower classes, but the aristocracy were also familiar with them. This can be seen by short remarks in the manuals, but becomes clearer in another text from aristocratic circles: the *Livre des seyntz medicines* (1354) of Henry of Grosmont, the first Duke of Lancaster.[33] In this book Henry describes the sinner as someone with seven wounds (in his ears, eyes, nose, mouth, hands, feet and heart – because they are the means with which to sin) and he suggests the sinner should be cured by medicines that are related to the death and resurrection of Christ and the sacraments of the Church. However, Henry departs regularly from this medical metaphor and one of his digressions is an unusually detailed representation of a fox hunt. Sloth is the vixen, as idleness is the root of all other vices. She mates with Pride, the most important of all the Deadly Sins, and together they produce five cubs, the other Deadly Sins. They live in the human heart, a corner of the foxes' den (i.e., the body). They are hunted and killed by the hunter or game warden (i.e., the confessor), who not only wants to destroy the foxes but also to protect other game (i.e., the virtues). He is helped by dogs. When one dog is sent into the foxes' den, he represents the conscience. When several dogs are used for a *par force* hunt, they represent the five senses that may discern sins. The result of their efforts is that the foxes are driven out into the open and killed. Their pelts are displayed in the castle hall: a repentant sinner should not hide his sins but should show them for what they are – wrong. Henry describes three methods to catch foxes and divides each method into three

parts. The first method is stopping up the entrances to the fox holes. This is done by true confession, full repentance and a strong will to do good. The second method is smoking out the fox. This is done with three fires. The first fire is the Holy Spirit and the smoke it produces is humility. The second fire is love towards Christ and its smoke is charity. The third fire is the fire of Hell and its smoke is cleanliness. The third method is to prod into a fox hole with a stick made up of three branches. These form a repetition, with a small variation, of an earlier element, since they are true confession, mournful repentance and firm hope of mercy. This digression shows that a member of the highest aristocratic circles knew not only the *par force* hunt but also the 'vulgar' ways of hunting foxes very well. It also shows that practical elements from daily life can be used to present religious instruction through allegoresis.

That allegoresis was possible we can also see in the manuals themselves. *Les livres du roy Modus et de la royne Ratio* consists of two parts. In the first part an apprentice asks King Method how to hunt all the individual beasts and the king answers. In the second part Queen Reason goes over the same material and interprets it allegorically.[34] A remarkable aspect of her chapter about the fox is that the fox is mostly indicated by the proper name Renart (see p. 8). Queen Reason says that he is a small animal with a red pelt and a long tail, a malicious appearance, deep-set eyes and small ears. He is full of wickedness towards all animals. Then Reason relates the anecdote of the fox who feigns death to lure the birds of prey that we know from Isidore's *Etymologies* and the bestiary tradition (cf. Figure 11). Here the fox is interpreted as those people who pretend to be pious to extort money from others. They steal from God with the help of maliciousness and deceit. Renart is full of malice, cunning, deceit, rapacity and all forms of wickedness. However, he has influenced the whole world. His behaviour is respected because it is so agreeable that most of the people follow it. In all three estates (clergy, nobility and peasants) people live according to his doctrine – not everyone, but many.

Figure 11. *Illustration in a copy of the* Livre de la chasse *by Gaston Phébus (Los Angeles, J. Paul Getty Museum, Ms. 27 (87. MR.34), fol. 27r; c.1430–40), showing in the upper half a woman with distaff, pursuing a fox (literature) and in the lower half a fox feigning death (bestiary). This illustration shows, just as the words of Queen Reason, that in the medieval image of the fox all types of idea can be combined.*

Lawyers in ecclesiastical and secular law are skilled in his science and read his guidelines daily. The same is true for holders of high royal and ecclesiastical offices. So even in the most practical of the genres discussed, an allegorical interpretation is possible. It is also important to note that, according to queen Reason, the fox's behaviour is very often practised in human society.

CONCLUSION

This chapter shows just how consistent the medieval scholarly view of the fox is. The same elements return again and again. This is especially true for the fox feigning death. The fox is almost always seen in a negative light: he is cunning, deceiving, malicious and corrupting. And so the scholarly view of the fox goes well with the religious view. Finally, this chapter demonstrates how interwoven the practical and allegorical approaches of reality were in the Middle Ages.

CHAPTER 3

THE FOX AND MEDIEVAL LITERATURE

THE MEDIEVAL STORIES about Reynard the fox are a new phenomenon in the literary history of Western Europe. The only type of animal story that we find in classical antiquity is the fable, to which the first section of this chapter is dedicated. The following three sections describe the development and richness of the medieval Reynard stories. Their development is sketched, first in general, then with special attention to *Reynaerts historie* – the source of all the early modern fox stories in Western Europe. Then it is shown how the same plot can be used to produce a fable, a short story and a part of a larger whole and how it can be used to achieve different effects. And because this is not a book about literary history but about foxes, the last section describes how Reynard, his wife Hermeline and their sons are portrayed in the separate strands of the tradition.

FABLES

The medieval fable tradition is large.[1] A catalogue of the medieval Latin and German fables lists 655 different fables.[2] In eighty-one of these a fox plays a role, so he is a frequent fable animal; however, those eighty-one fables do not give a coherent image of the fox, as is the case, for example, in encyclopaedias. The meaning of a fable arises from the situation it describes, which determines the interpretation. The animals are not fully fledged characters but rather actors whose exact part and meaning varies in accordance with the desired situation. Hence there is great diversity in the presentation of the various animals and so a sketch of the fox in fables can only be general and will show inconsistencies.

In medieval fables the fox is frequently presented as Reynard and not as an anonymous fox, as is traditional in fables (see this book pp. 8–9). Hence, the distinction between fables and other animal stories is in medieval practice less clear than in modern theoretical reflections. However, the most remarkable (although not the most surprising) element of the fables in which a fox appears is that they all deal with elements such as insight, shrewdness, understanding or wisdom. This is most conspicuous in the *Speculum sapientiae*, an original medieval fable collection.[3] It is divided into four books and each book handles a cardinal virtue (prudence, justice, fortitude and temperance). The first book is dedicated to faults against prudence and shows many examples of foolishness and self-conceit. In this book the fox appears in one-third of all the fables. In the other books he appears noticeably less often.[4] In fables there is therefore also a clear connection between the fox and shrewdness. However, this shrewdness is judged in quite different ways.

There are fables in which the fox is regarded positively, for example, the fable about the vixen and the eagle or the one about the sick lion and the fox.[5] In the first fable an eagle has stolen some fox cubs. The mother asks for them back, but her request is refused. She then sets fire to the tree in which the eagle nests and by this ruse she manages to get her children back. In the second fable, a sick lion is lying is his den. He devours all animals that come inside to visit him. When the fox comes, he refuses to enter because he can see tracks going in but no tracks coming out again. In these cases, the fox uses shrewdness to help himself. He does no harm to others out of ill will.

There are also fables in which the image of the fox is ambiguous, especially in the *Speculum sapientiae*. In this book, an anecdote in which the fox praises the cock for his singing and his knowledge and then asks whether he may kiss him is told as a fable.[6] The cock lets himself be deceived and is grabbed by the throat. He characterises this behaviour as bad, which the fox denies. It is correct to punish the proud and the cock's bad luck is caused by his own excessive pride. This moral is understandable in a context dedicated to criticism of pride, but the fox's words are no real excuse for his behaviour. We find the same ambiguity when we are told how the fox pretended to be dead.[7] The prey he is trying to lure is the raven. However, the latter is not deceived. The two start a conversation in which the raven impresses upon the fox that desires drive out wisdom. The fox answers that he learned that long ago, but that at times everyone makes mistakes. He continues with a speech on the alertness that wisdom requires. Here the fox is thus at the same time a negative example and the mouthpiece for a true and correct moral message.

And finally, there are fables in which the fox is portrayed as a purely negative character. A clear example is the fable of the fox and the crane or stork (Figure 12).[8] The fox invites the crane for dinner but presents the food on a flat plate

so that the crane can only take small bites. In revenge the crane invites the fox for dinner and presents the food in high vases so that the fox is unable to get at it. This behaviour of the fox is always seen as negative. His shrewdness is used here to spite another, and it is fitting that he receives the same treatment afterwards.

Many fables, however, show behaviour that can be interpreted in both a positive and a negative way. A clear example is the fable of the fox who saw grapes but could not reach them and then decided that this was just as well because they were still unripe.[9] This is interpreted positively when the moral states that it is wise not to wish for what cannot be had, and negatively when the moral states that a bad person speaks evil when he cannot do evil. Another example is the fable of the she-ape who asked a fox for a part of his tail to cover her naked behind.[10] The fox refuses. This can be interpreted positively when the moral states that it is wise not to give away what you need yourself, and negatively when the moral states that in the same way the rich refuse to help the poor.

Figure 12. *Fable of the fox and the stork. Breviary of Louis of Male* (Brussels, KBR [Royal Library], 9427), *fol. 62v. Second half fourteenth century.* © KBR.

Some fable collections demonstrate in their content that they were meant for a specific public, this is certainly true of the fables of Marie de France.[11] Marie's works were written in the twelfth century in the French of the Anglo-Norman nobility in England. Many of her fables relate to courtly or feudal values. In two of them the fox plays a role. The first is fable 89.[12] Here, nobody can make peace between a wolf and a fox. In the end they bring their disagreement before the king, who hears the cases but does not give a verdict because he does not want to decide between their pleas. He trusts neither of them:

> Sa (= the wolf's) mençunge est plus convenable
> E meuz resemble chose estable
> Que del gupil la veritez. (ll. 15–17)

> For lies and wolf are consonant!
> Lies better suit his temperament
> Than truth does fox's disposition.[13]

This fable states that it is not natural for a fox to speak the truth, implying that foxes are normally seen as liars. The moral rejects the king's behaviour:

> Issi deit fere li bon sire:
> Il ne deit pas juger ne dire,
> Si si hume, que de lui tienent,
> Ireement en sa curt vienent.
> Ne deit si vers l'un parler,
> Que a l'autre deive mut peser,
> Mes adrescer a sun poër
> E l'ire fere remaner. (ll. 19–26)

No good seignior should be this way:
No judgment pass, no verdict say,
If men under his sovereignty
Should come to court most angrily.
Unto the one he must not utter
Something that might upset the other.
But he must try to put things right,
As best he can, and end their spite.

In a certain way this fable and its moral refer to the problem raised in many branches of the *Roman de Renart*. Here, it is stated that a good lord brings peace between his vassals when they disagree. In many branches there is a conflict between fox and wolf, but it is seldom solved, and never in a way that ends their spite. Sometimes this is caused by the king's unwillingness to decide, but very often the adversaries simply refuse to reconcile. Their conflict is unresolvable, just as it is presented here. The fact that we find this theme in a fable and in Reynard stories suggests that it was an important issue in the courtly societies of the twelfth century.

The theme of fable 99 – the fox and the cat – is companionship, an important 'horizontal' ideal of courtly society (Figure 13).[14] A fox and a cat decide to be good companions. The cat asks the fox how he would defend himself if danger were to come. The fox answers that he has a bag full of tricks and that he will choose the best one. The cat answers that in that case they cannot be companions because he knows only one trick. Then two dogs attack them and the fox asks the cat for help, but the cat refuses: 'Aïe tei! / N'ai que un engin, cel ert od mei!' ('You must your own help be / I've

Figure 13. *Fable of the fox and the cat. The cat is safe in the tree, the fox is caught by dogs.* Woodcut from Reynke de Vos (*Lübeck* 1498), *the Low German adaptation of* Reynaerts historie; *fol.* K1r.

but one trick, and it's for me!') (ll. 21–2). The cat hides in a thornbush, but the fox is grabbed by the dogs. The cat urges the fox to open his bag, but the fox answers that it is already too late and that he would have preferred to have the cat's trick. And the moral is:

> Del menteür avient suvent:
> Tut parot il raisnablement,
> Sil put li sages entreprendre.
> Del leial humme est meuz creüe,
> Une parole e entendue,
> E plus put en un grant pleit,
> Que quanque li mentere feit. (ll. 41–8)

> With lying men the same is found:
> However logical they sound,
> A sage can trip them up, if he
> But listens to them carefully.
> An honest man is held more true,
> His words more often heeded, too,
> More suasive in a legal case
> Than anything a liar says.

The fox is presented here not as a boaster but as a liar, so his image in these two fables is consistent. He is twice linked with lying and with being untrustworthy in a legal context. From a modern perspective, the behaviour of the cat can be seen as ambiguous because he only takes care of himself. However, before the danger arrives, he announces that the fox and he are too different to be good companions and his behaviour can be seen as self-reliance. When one assumes that in dangerous situations self-help is the best help, the cat's behaviour is understandable and prudent. This is the dominant medieval interpretation.

There are many fable collections for preachers. In some of them the fables do not conclude with a moral, as is usual, but with a detailed allegorical interpretation of individual features of the story.[15] This type of interpretation links these fables to Bible exegesis and the bestiaries, which use the same technique. An important representative of this tradition is Odo of Cheriton, a thirteenth-century English cleric.[16] When he tells the fable of the fox and the cat, he calls the fox Reinardus and the cat Tebergo, which shows that he is influenced by Reynard stories. He characterises this fable as *contra aduocatos* (against lawyers) and gives the following moral:

Per catum intellegimus simplices qui nesciunt nisi unicum artificium, scilicet salire in caelum. Per Reinardum intelligimus aduocatos, causidicos, fraudulentos, qui habent XVII fraudes, insuper sacculum plenum. Veniunt uenatores et canes infernales et uenantur homines; sed iusti in celum saliunt; impii, fraudulenti a demonibus capiuntur, et tunc potest iustus dicere: Reinarde, Reinarde, aperi sacculum tuum; omnes fraudes tue non poterunt te liberare a dentibus et manibus demoniorum.[17]

By the cat we understand simple people who only know one single skill, that is to jump into heaven [as the cat in the fable jumped into a tree]. By Reynard we mean advocates, lawyers, fraudulent people, who have seventeen types of frauds in their full bag. Hunters and infernal dogs come, and they hunt men; the good men leap into heaven; the ungodly, the deceitful are taken by the Devils, and then the just may say: 'Reynard, Reynard, open your bag; all your deceits will not be able to free you from the teeth and the hands of the demons.'

Here the fox allegorically represents fraudulent lawyers and advocates. There is thus again a link between the fox and injustice. We have seen this interpretation in Bible exegesis too (see p. 33), but the dominant allegorical meaning of the fox there was the Devil, and this is also true in these allegorising fables. The fable of the knight and the snake,[18] however, gives another, exceptional interpretation. A knight passes two fighting snakes. The losing snake asks the knight's help and the knight gives it. But when this snake is safe, it tries to strangle the knight in order to eat

him. The knight protests, but the snake says that its behaviour is perfectly normal. The judgement of three animals will prove this. The first two animals, a bovine and a horse, agree with the snake that it is indeed normal to repay good with evil. The third animal, a fox, however, wants to see the original situation restored before he gives his judgement. When the knight is safe on his horse, with his lance in his hand, the snake on the ground is no longer a threat and the fox advises the knight to freely ride away. In the allegorical interpretation this is said about the fox:

> quid dicit prudens Vulpes, id est Christus, per David? Cum accepero tempus, ego iusticias iudicabo [cf. Ps. 74:3]. Iste Vulpes in rubea pelle, per stigmata passionis sue, in die iudicij separavit oves ab [h]edis [cf. Matt. 25:32], serpentes a militibus, id est tales filios diaboli a suis fidelibus.[19]

> what says the wise Fox, i.e. Christ, by (the words of) David? When I think the time is right, I shall judge the judges. This fox with his red pelt, by the signs of his passion, shall separate on the day of judgment the sheep from the goats, the snakes from the knights, i.e. such children of the Devil from his faithful.

This interpretation may be surprising, but it respects the principles of Bible exegesis. Every creature has as many allegorical meanings as it has properties, so everything can be interpreted *in bonam partem* ('in a good way') or *in malam partem* ('in a negative way'). The context determines what is the most fitting interpretation. Here the red pelt of the fox is linked to the blood that Christ shed for our sins, so this is an interpretation *in bonam partem*. From a medieval perspective this is a correct interpretation, but it is a unique one. I know of no other interpretation of a fox that is *in bonam partem*.

THE DEVELOPMENT OF THE REYNARD STORIES

The Reynard stories were 'invented' in the Middle Ages.[20] The first text in which a fox was given a name (Reinardus) is the Latin *Ysengrimus*. This text was written in Ghent in 1148 or 1149, but we know that some stories and motifs we find represented here are older because images remain from some of its stories that are older than the *Ysengrimus* (see p. 12) and we have still earlier written experiments with stories that we also find in the *Ysengrimus*.[21] This is especially true of the stories of the sick lion and of the fox and the cock.

The first story relates that the king falls ill.[22] All the animals, except the fox, come to show their grief and to suggest remedies. One of the animals (most often the wolf, sometimes the bear) tries to get the fox convicted for treason because of her absence (*vulpes* is feminine, see p. 11). The fox is warned, comes to court and says that she was absent until now because she had sought for a way to help the king. To be cured he must wrap himself in the hide of the fox's accuser. This happens, the fox mocks the flayed beast and the king recovers. We find this story in some Latin fable collections, in a separate Latin story from the ninth century and in the *Ecbasis captivi* (mid-eleventh century, probably written in the Vosges region).[23] That all animals come to the king's court with exception of the fox becomes an important

theme in vernacular fox stories, but the reason for the gathering changes. The animals come because the king wants to do justice, not because he is ill. (We can already see a nascent form of this element in the *Ecbasis* and the *Ysengrimus*.)

The oldest version of the story of the cock and the fox that we know of is a poem by Alcuin, one of Charlemagne's most important advisers (*c*.735–804), although he tells it about a cock and a wolf.[24] It is fleshed out in the *Ysengrimus*, it becomes the opening part of the oldest branch of the *Roman de Renart* and its best-known version in English is Chaucer's *Nun's Priest's Tale*.[25] In its fully fledged form it narrates how a fox meets a cock, admires his voice, but says that the cock's father sang more impressively because he closed his eyes while singing. The cock closes his eyes to surpass his father and is grabbed by the fox who runs away. He is pursued by farmers who want the cock back. They call the fox 'thief'. The cock advises the fox to reply that he got his prey lawfully. The fox does this and when he opens his mouth, the cock escapes. This story is a classic example of 'the trickster tricked'.

The *Ysengrimus* is a fascinating story, and in it the fox Reinardus is presented as a brilliant orator, but the main protagonist is the wolf. This is true for the whole of the Latin tradition. It seems as if the fox as central character is linked to the vernacular. The vernacular Reynard tradition starts with the French *Roman de Renart*.[26] This name was given in the Middle Ages to several collections of stories. The word *Roman* does not have the meaning of the modern French word 'roman', which means 'novel', but rather, it indicates that it concerns stories in the vernacular, not in Latin. The separate stories are called branches by their medieval authors, and this is an apt metaphor because we never see a unified whole (the tree) but always parts (the branches) that are combined in ever new and different ways. The oldest manuscripts containing these collections date from the thirteenth century, but most of the separate branches must have been composed earlier.[27] It is generally accepted that the oldest written branch was the work of a certain Pierre de Saint-Cloud (of whom we know nothing more than his name), that it consisted of a combination of the manuscript parts that today are mostly characterised as II and Va and that it was written between 1174 and 1177.[28] In the period before 1200, fourteen other branches were written. Twelve more branches, which are mostly considered as epigone work, were written in the first half of the thirteenth century. This material shows influence from the *Ysengrimus* and other parts of the Latin tradition, but also from oral tradition. It is impossible to determine the precise relations between all the parts of the manuscripts that are left but together they show the richness and the variety of a tradition that must have functioned for at least two centuries in an interaction between written and oral versions.

There are two main themes in the branches of the *Roman de Renart*: the quest for food and the quest for justice.[29] We find the first theme mainly in stories that resemble fables. They describe the meeting of two animals. One of them, most often the fox, tries to eat the other. The story of cock and fox, described above, is a good example of this type. The other theme is handled in stories in which the animals form a society. This society is restricted to the nobility. This differs from the Latin tradition because the *Ysengrimus*, the *Ecbasis* and many other Latin beast stories are situated in

monastic circles. The quest for justice in this noble society is most often that of Isengrin the wolf, who is at war with Renart. His main accusation against Renart is that the fox raped his wife, Hersent. This is a complicated case because there are two meetings between fox and she-wolf that must be taken into consideration. The first is in the wolf's den. The fox arrives there by accident and when Hersent asks why he has not visited her earlier, he answers that he did not dare to because her husband is everywhere complaining that they committed adultery together. The she-wolf is furious. When her husband accuses her falsely, he deserves to be cuckolded. And she invites Renart to have sex with her. When Isengrin hears about this he is very angry, but after a while the wolves reconcile and promise each other that they will capture Renart when it is possible. When the wolves see Renart, they pursue the fox and Hersent is faster than Isengrin. Renart flies into his den. Hersent tries to follow him but gets stuck in the opening. Renart comes out through another exit and this time he rapes the immobilised she-wolf, under the eyes of her husband.[30] These two scenes give rise to many debates: was it rape or adultery, is illicit love acceptable, should there be a complaint about this, and so on. These discussions are presided over by King Noble, the lion. And just as Isengrin never succeeds in getting his rightful revenge for Renart's misdeeds, so Noble never succeeds in disciplining Renart. These stories can be very critical about courts and the meting out of justice, but mostly they aim at humour and satire more than at serious social criticism. Some of the later branches, however, show Renart in a more negative light. He is no longer a prankster or trickster (see pp. 9–10) but someone who is power hungry and who does not shy away from the most hideous crimes to reach his goal.

This new view of Reynard's character is taken over and further developed in epic stories. The oldest of these is a German text, *Reinhart Fuchs*. It was written at the end of the twelfth century in Alsace by an author who, in the text, calls himself Heinrich der Glîchezâre ('the hypocrite'). The text consists of three parts, all three based on branches of the *Roman de Renart*. The first part describes the fox's meetings with small animals. The fox tries to grab them to eat them, but he never succeeds. In the second part we find a series of confrontations between the fox and the wolf, the she-wolf and their children. This time the fox is mostly successful and he hurts the wolves several times. In the third part the fox comes to the court of the sick king. He manipulates the king by promising to heal him, but instead he wreaks havoc on the existing order by poisoning the king and then leaving the court. The king dies. In this story the fox is a very negative figure and one could say that he destroys the social order.

In French this negative fox became the main character of two texts, which both stem from the County of Flanders. The first of these is *Le Couronnement de Renart* (1263–70). In this story Renart tries to become king with help from the Franciscans and the Dominicans. Disguised as cleric, he goes to court and prophesies a change of ruler. Noble is already ill and this is too much for him: he dies and Renart becomes king. The pope invites him to Rome and there he teaches all the cardinals his craft. After that, they use it always. In this text Renart becomes the master wielder of all reprehensible worldly political misdeeds.

In *Renart le Nouvel*, written in 1289 by Jacquemart Gielée in Lille, the vision of the character of Renart is bleaker still. He becomes the allegorical representation of all that is bad and sinful in the world. The story is divided into two books that both describe a conflict between Renart and Noble. Noble is originally linked to the virtues but when he makes his peace with Renart, they disappear and only the vices, represented by Renart, remain in the world. Then a new theme is introduced: criticism of the preaching orders. Renart's sons become head of the Dominicans and the Franciscans and Renart himself of both the Templars and the Hospitallers. Fortuna offers Renart the place on top of her wheel and promises him that she will stop it when he is seated and since then Renart has reigned supreme in the world.

The last French text is *Renart le Contrefait*. It was written in the first half of the fourteenth century by an author from Troyes. Just like the *Roman de Renart*, it consists of a loose series of branches. Its second version contained more than 40,000 lines. Its erudition is staggering and its world view very bleak.

THE MAKING OF A BESTSELLER

The most famous and most popular branch of the *Roman de Renart* was probably branch I. It opens most of the collections. This branch provided not only the basis for the third part of *Reinhart Fuchs*, but also for a Middle Dutch text, *Van den vos Reynaerde*, which is today considered by many scholars as the pinnacle of the genre. *Van den vos Reynaerde* was written around the middle of the thirteenth century in or in the vicinity of Ghent.[31] The story narrates that King Nobel the lion, had proclaimed a meeting of his court. All animals were present with the exception of Reynaert. He is accused by Ysegrim the wolf of raping Hersint the she-wolf, by the little dog Cortois of stealing a sausage, and by Pancer the beaver of attacking Kuwaert the hare, but he is defended by his nephew Grimbeert the badger. The defence seems successful but then the corpse of the hen Coppe appears, who has been murdered by Reynaert, and the fox's guilt is now undeniable. He is summoned three times to appear before the court. The first two summoners, Bruun the bear and Tibeert the tomcat, he lures into a trap by playing on their greed (he promises Bruun honey and Tibeert mice). Mutilated, they return to the court. With the third summoner, Grimbeert, Reynaert comes to court where he is sentenced to death.

Thus far the story follows broadly the plot of branch I. In that branch, Renart then falls at Noble's feet and says that he wishes to atone for his sins with a pilgrimage to the Holy Land, to fight there against the infidels. Noble pities him and – after a plea from Grimbert –allows him to depart and gives him a crusader's cross and a pilgrim's scrip and staff for his journey. After leaving the court Renart meets Coart the hare, who had thrown stones at him during the sentencing. In revenge, Renart now seizes him as food for his young. From a distance he mocks the king and his court by wiping his backside with the crusader's cross and throwing it to the king. Coart uses this opportunity to escape. Enraged, the whole court pursues the fox, but in the nick of time Renart manages to reach the safety of his castle of Malpertuis. While this part of the story is told with much pace and verve and is clearly satirical in tone, to the modern reader Noble's

volte-face seems surprising. The narrative gives no clear indication as to why he should suddenly abandon his hostility to Renart, so the events seem fairly random and have no internal consistency. It would seem that the author of *Van den vos Reynaerde* was also dissatisfied with this. At any event, from this point on, he deviates from his source and begins to tell his own story.

After being convicted Reynaert asks permission to make a public confession and in the course of this he casually mentions a treasure and a conspiracy on the king's life. In exchange for this treasure the king forgives Reynaert and helps him to go on a pilgrimage (see pp. 42–4). Reynaert leaves the court with Bellijn the ram and Kuwaert the hare. Back in his den he murders the latter, hides his head in his pilgrim's scrip, and sends that back to court with Bellijn. He himself leaves with his wife and children for the wilderness. When the king sees Kuwaert's head, he realises that he has been deceived and is furious. On the advice of the leopard Firapeel he makes his peace with Ysegrim and Bruun and offers them Bellijn and all his kind in compensation. On the surface, at least, the peace has been restored.

Van den vos Reynaerde seems to have been a popular story in the Middle Ages. In any case, the remaining manuscripts are spread over the whole area of the Low Countries.[32] But at some moment at the end of the fourteenth or, more probably, in the first decades of the fifteenth century, an author linked to the patrician family Van Diksmuide was nevertheless unhappy with the story because he decided to rewrite it.[33] This author wrote a bipartite story. The first part retells *Van den vos Reynaerde* faithfully, but with many small changes that often foreshadow the new second part.

The end, however, is changed completely. When Reynaert announces that he wants to leave Nobel's realm, his wife protests. She wants to stay in Malpertuus and Reynaert gives in. This is necessary as preparation for the second part. The king prolongs the meeting of his court and during the festivities Reynaert is accused anew. Grimbeert goes again to Malpertuus and Reynaert comes for the second time with his nephew to court. Again, he states that he is innocent and a faithful servant of the king. The king is not impressed and expresses his wish to hang Reynaert. The fox is so afraid that he has no immediate response, but the she-ape Rukenau comes to his rescue. She calms the king and makes it clear that Reynaert has been very useful to him in the past and has much support among the animals of the realm. The king is now willing to listen to Reynaert again. The fox says that he did not send Kuwaert's head to court, but three jewels, taken from the stolen treasure: a ring for the king and a comb and a mirror for the queen. This second treasure story works as well as the first one. Almost everyone believes him, and the king and queen want him to go on a quest to retrieve them. Only Ysegrim the wolf is not deceived. He tries to make it clear that the fox is a criminal and a liar, but he cannot compete with the fox with words, so in the end he asks for a duel. Reynaert accepts and with help of very dirty tricks he wins. The king makes him one of his highest officers and asks for his support and counsel in the future. The epilogue states that the fox still has this central position in all courts, secular and ecclesiastical. *Van den vos Reynaerde* was a story in which the king acted unlawfully but tried to redress his mistakes. *Reynaerts historie* is a story in which the king places a criminal in a position of power

because that criminal is useful to him; another, but far more damaging, sign of egotism.

In the second half of the fifteenth century *Reynaerts historie* was printed twice by Gheraert Leeu, one of the most important printers in the Low Countries. In 1479 he printed *Reynaerts historie* in a prose rendering in Gouda. Between 1487 and 1490, after his firm transferred to Antwerp, Leeu printed *Reynaerts historie* again, this time respecting the original verse form, but dividing the text into chapters and adding a moral to each chapter.[34]

These two Dutch books were the starting point of a European tradition.[35] Variant versions of Leeu's prose text were printed in the Low Countries until the nineteenth century. Two of them were translated into French and printed until the eighteenth century. Leeu's prose text was also the source for Caxton's *History of Reynard the Fox* (1481). Caxton's version was the starting point of an English tradition in Britain and Ireland that lasts until the present day. Leeu's verse version was the source for *Reynke de vos*, a Low German version printed in Lübeck in 1498. In 1544 a High German version appeared and in 1567 this High German version was translated into Latin; in 1706 this Latin version was translated into English so that since then England has had two distinct but related Reynard traditions. The Low German version was also translated into Danish in 1555 and this Danish version led to a Swedish and an Icelandic one. Most of the versions mentioned were reprinted often, so in the early modern period we find *Reynaerts historie* – in its variant forms – all over Europe. And in more recent times it had still more success. The Low German text also led, via a number of intermediate stages, to Goethe's *Reineke Fuchs* (1794), a version in Germanic hexameters. As part of Goethe's *opera omnia*, this *Reineke Fuchs* established a tradition of its own. It was translated into French, English, Dutch, Spanish, Hungarian, Russian and Japanese among other languages. Of all the medieval Reynard stories, *Reynaerts historie* has become by far the most successful, widespread and enduring bestseller.

VARIATIONS

The previous sections have shown implicitly that the same situation or the same motif can be used by different authors in different ways. This phenomenon is so important that it deserves explicit treatment, so this section is dedicated to the ways in which the motif of the fox and the wolf in the well has been handled in medieval literature.[36]

This motif or plot is built around the mechanism of a pulley with a rope with a bucket at each end, so that as one bucket rises, the other goes down (Figure 14). The oldest surviving texts in which this motif plays a role were written by Rabbi Rashi from Troyes (c.1070) and Petrus Alphonsus, a converted Spanish Jew (between 1109 and 1114).[37] Both texts are a two-part fable-exemplum.

Rabbi Rashi first tells how the fox tricked the wolf into doing something stupid on a Sabbath evening, and then leads him at night, under a full moon, to a well. The fox jumps into the upper bucket and goes down. When the wolf asks why he has done this, the fox points to the reflection of the moon and calls it cheese. The wolf also wants part of the 'cheese' and the fox advises him to get into the other bucket. When he does this, the wolf goes down and the fox gets up. When the wolf asks how this is possible, the fox

Figure 14. *The end of the well episode: the fox escaping (right) and the wolf hauled up from the well (and afterwards beaten) by a human (left). Drawing for unfinished marginal decoration. Cambridge, Fitzwilliam Museum, 298, fol. 138v (c.1302–16). © The Fitzwilliam Museum, Cambridge.*

quotes two Bible verses in his answer: 'just balances, just weights' (Lev. 19:36) and 'the righteous man is delivered out of trouble, and the wicked person comes in his stead' (Prov. 11:8). These quotations must be meant ironically because the buckets are not just and the fox is not righteous. Rabbi Rashi wrote this fable in the context of commentary on the Talmud,[38] so its main aim was probably a ludic use of Bible verses, as a 'counterweight' to their normal use in the Talmud.

Petrus Alphonus first tells how a fox offers to settle a conflict between a farmer and a wolf over the ownership of oxen. The fox asks the farmer for two hens as a fee for a positive verdict and then offers the wolf an enormous cheese as compensation for the oxen. The wolf accepts and the fox brings him to a well in which they see the reflection of the full moon. The fox urges the wolf to go down and eat his fill, but the wolf refuses and commands the fox to bring the 'cheese' to him. The fox goes down in a bucket, cries at the bottom that the cheese is too heavy and that he needs help. The wolf gets into the other bucket and, by his greater weight, rescues the fox from the well. The moral is that one should not give up something in the hope of getting something better in its stead. This very pragmatic attitude is often found in exempla.

This motif of going down and up in the well was later used to create comic stories. The clearest examples are the two versions in the *Roman de Renart* (date uncertain and *c.*1178) and the Middle English *The Fox and the Wolf* (around 1300).[39] That these stories were meant to be comic is proven, for instance, by the prologue of the most frequent of the *Roman de Renart* versions. This begins:

> Or me covient tel cose dire
> Don't je vous puis tout faire rire
> Car je sais bien, çou est la pure,
> Que de sermon n'avés vous cure
> Ne de cor saint oïr la vie:
> De ce ne vous prent nule envie,
> Mais de tel cose qui vous plaise.[40]

I now have something to tell you that should make you laugh; for the truth is, as I know well, that you have no wish for a sermon or to hear the life of some holy saint. What you want is not all that, but something to amuse you.[41]

The following story tells first how Renart finds food and then that he is thirsty. He finds a deep well and looks into it. He sees his own reflection and thinks that it is Hermeline, his wife. He puts his feet in the upper bucket and goes down. In the water he realises his mistake. Then Isengrin arrives at the well, looks into it and sees Renart and his own reflection, which he interprets as Hersent, his wife. He abuses his wife for what he sees as adultery. Renart asks who is calling and says that he is dead. Isengrin pities him, but Renart says he is delighted because he is now in the heavenly paradise, a perfect place:

> Caiens sont les gaaigneries,
> Li bos, li plain, les praieries;
> Ciens a riche poucinaille;
> Ciens puet on veoir mainte ouaille
> Et mainte oe et mainte chievre;
> Ciens puet on veoir maint lievre
> Et bues et vaiches et moutons,
> Espriviers, ostours et faucons![42]

> Here are the farmsteads, the woods, the plains, the meadows; here there are great riches; and there is a great quantity of cattle to be seen here, many ewes and goats, and you can see an abundance of hares, bullocks, cows, and sheep, sparrowhawks, goshawks, and falcons.[43]

Isengrin wants to be there, too. Renart answers that only good people can come into paradise, and that Isengrin's negative feelings about Renart hinder him from entering. Immediately, Isengrin forgives Renart for the rape of his wife. Renart says to Isengrin that the buckets are the balance for weighing good and evil. When the good is heavy enough, it will come down and the evil will stay behind. After checking whether Isengrin has confessed, and after a prayer, Isengrin is allowed to test the 'balance'. He jumps into the upper bucket and owing to his greater weight he goes down and Renart comes up. When they pass each other, Isengrin asks what is happening and Renart answers:

> Quant li uns va, li autres vient,
> C'est la costume qui avient!
> Je vois en paradis la sus
> Et tu vas en enfer la jus![44]

> When one comes down, the other comes up: that's the normal procedure. I'm going up there to Paradise, and you're going down into Hell.[45]

The story ends with a description of how Isengrin is hauled up by monks and gets a severe beating, but escapes in the end and recovers at home.

The comic element in this story has several levels. The first is the misinterpretation of a reflection. By changing the reflection of the moon into the reflection of the characters, it became possible to link this story to the sexual relationship between the fox and the she-wolf that is a central theme in many Reynard stories. The second is the relationship between the fox and the wolf. The wolf is aggrieved with Renart because the fox raped his wife, but when this resentment hinders him in the pursuit of food, he forgives the fox immediately. Renart is the cleverer of the two and

uses the wolf's gullibility to save himself from a dire situation. The third is the play with religious elements. Of course, heavenly Paradise is up and not down, and it does not consist of all the earthly abundance that Renart describes. It is a nice touch that Renart reverses his location of Paradise when he is saved, and his view of Paradise changes, too: it is no longer a landscape with an abundance of food, but a place where one is free to go where one wants. It is not clear whether this comic story also has a message, but if it has one, it is Renart's characterisation 'when one comes down, the other comes up'. The situation in the world changes continually and when you are clever, you can influence this process.

The Fox and the Wolf follows the plot of the French story closely, but elaborates on some elements, especially the dialogue between the fox and the wolf. The element of confession illustrates this well. In the French text the wolf says that he has already confessed to an old hare and a she-goat. In the English text, the fox says that the wolf cannot enter the well before he has confessed. There is no one else available, so the wolf asks the fox to hear his confession. The fox first refuses, but eventually gives in. The wolf confesses that he has eaten 1,000 sheep and has often has spoken badly of the fox because he thought that he had a sexual relationship with his wife. He thought this because he had seen them together in bed, but his eyes must have betrayed him. So, an element that is mentioned only in the French text is elaborated in the English text, creating the outrageous situation where the victim must beg the culprit for forgiveness that he thought badly of him. There is no explicit message in the text, but perhaps it shows the public that there are characters who can let the 'reality' that they create with their words dominate the actual situation.[46]

The motif is also used in allegorising fables. Odo of Cheriton, for instance, tells it in a very economical way.[47] He simply relates the events and makes the words of the fox more believable by letting him say only that he has eaten lots of fish. He ends by telling the reader that the wolf was pulled out of the well by peasants (not monks – Odo was a cleric) who killed him. In the allegoresis the fox and the peasants are interpreted as the Devil and the wolf as the stupid man who goes down into the well of guilt because he wishes for worldly goods.

The Scottish schoolmaster Robert Henryson (second half of the fifteenth century), however, uses more than 200 verses in his *Moral Fabillis of Esope the Phrygian* to retell the Petrus Alphonsus version.[48] He fleshes out Petrus' short and succinct story with descriptions and by adding considerable dialogue. His allegoresis (called *Moralitas*) is very elaborate. He interprets the wolf as the wicked man who oppresses the poor (because the wolf wants to take the oxen from the farmer). The fox is the Devil because he induces everyone to do something bad, and the farmer is a godly man because he is willing to give up his hens, which are works that are based on faith. The cheese is interpreted as avarice because it is the wish for worldly goods that drives people to jump into the well, which is Hell. We see here that the allegorising technique can be combined with elaborate story telling. The allegorising of the separate elements is very consistent and is in line with what we find in other allegorising fables.

We also find the motif as part of a larger whole. It is one of the adventures that is told in *Renart le Contrefait*.[49]

With regard to the plot, this version resembles those of the *Roman de Renart* and *The Fox and the Wolf in the Well*, but it is far more verbose and the display of scholarship plays a big role, not only in this adventure but in the text as a whole. A clear example of this is that the single verse that Renart uses to describe to Isengrin what happens when they pass each other ('Quant li uns va, li autres vient') is enlarged here to twenty-two verses (p. 59, ll. 28177–98). And when Renart is down in the well, he reflects that Frobert the cricket (whom he had met before he came to the well) was right when he advised him to follow reason. The fox cites Cassiodorus and his warnings against pride. Humbled, he asks for the support of Reason (pp. 55–6, ll. 27825–82). Isengrin cites Salomon, Jesus Sirach, Cicero, Seneca and Petrus Alphonsus, among others, when he complains of his situation down in the well (pp. 59–60, ll. 28221–306). In *Renart le Contrefait* the adventures are an excuse for the display of erudition and all the quoting of authorities even seems a hindrance to any attempt to learn something from the actual situation.

The motif may also be found in the second part of *Reinhart Fuchs*, which relates how the fox interacts with the wolves.[50] It is part of a series of pranks that Reinhart plays on Isengrin and his wife. The plot is identical to that in the *Roman de Renart* but is reduced to the bare minimum. The aim is no longer to tell an amusing story but to show a series of events that explains the enmity between wolf and fox.

And lastly, the story is retold in *Reynaerts historie*.[51] Here it is part of the duel of words between the wolves and the fox, which takes place between the second treasure story and the real duel of wolf and fox. Two aspects in this version are unique: Reynaert's victim is the she-wolf and the anecdote is told not by a narrator but by the she-wolf herself, as a complaint against the fox. It is inspired by the *Roman de Renart* because it describes the system of the pulley and it contains the 'punchline' 'Het is der werlt loop … Dat een gaet op ende dander neder' ('In the world one rises and another goes down', ll. 6429–30). It is very short, however, and more realistic because Reynaert does not describe a paradise, but rather says that the well contains many fishes. Reynaert also answers the complaint: he did it reluctantly, but she could better bear the inevitable beating that would follow a release than he, and in this way she was warned not to trust others too easily.

So, this motif has been used in standalone stories and as episodes in larger works. It has been told in very different ways, as a separate story and as part of a larger whole. It has been used in a comic and a didactic way and with a pragmatic, amusing or religious aim. The versatility it shows is a characteristic attribute of the whole tradition.

REYNARD AND HIS FAMILY

The tradition of Reynard stories is long, broad and varied, so it is impossible to sketch a coherent image of Reynard and his family without inconsistencies. What follows is an outline of major tendencies without an attempt to find a non-existent unity.

In the beginning of the Reynard tradition, the *Ysengrimus*, the fox is single, which fits in with that text's concentration of on monastic topics. From the *Roman de Renart* onwards, Reynard has a wife, Hermeline, and children. Reynard is a trickster. He deceives others, mostly to profit from them, sometimes just for fun. His ruses very often

involve misuse of language. In the *Ysengrimus* he was presented as a master orator and in many parts of the later tradition he is described as someone who manipulates others by talking to them. The reasons for his deceptions vary. Sometimes he is just a prankster (many branches of the *Roman de Renart*), but he can also be a political power figure (*Couronnement de Renart*), evil incarnate (*Renart le Nouvel*) or the crafty courtier who knows everything about the struggle for influence at courts (*Reynaerts historie*). Let us now look more specifically at his relationships with wife and children.

Reynard's family in the stories seems to be designed to give him a stable 'starting point'. Many branches start with the fox leaving his home to obtain food for his hungry wife and children, but this aim is often forgotten when playing a trick on another animal or filling his own belly. He loves his children, but his own needs come first. He also loves his wife, but he is not true to her because he has sexual relationships with or rapes Hersent, the she-wolf and Fière, the queen.[52] He does this not only for his own bodily pleasure but also to spite their husbands.[53] In other words, he sees his family mainly as something that should contribute to his own well-being, and this determines his priorities; however, when he is at home, he behaves mostly as a good father and husband should. The disharmony that characterises the Isengrin-Hersent couple is absent in the Renart-Hermeline relationship.

Hermeline is normally portrayed very positively.[54] She is young, courtly, noble and sensible, a caring mother and wife. When Reynard returns wounded she nurses him back to health. When he returns unscathed she listens to his adventures, and when he brings food she and their children eat it. She advises her husband and when he is in need she comes to his rescue. At the end of the first part of *Reynaerts historie*, for instance, she advises against their leaving the realm of Nobel (making the second part possible) and at the end of branch Ia Reynard is at the point of being hanged when Hermeline arrives with a rich ransom. Because of her pleas and the presented riches, the king forgives the fox once again.

In most cases, the role of Hermeline is small. In two branches, however, it is more remarkable. In branch IX she first advises Renart to take revenge on the farmer Liétard by stealing the straps he uses to yoke his oxen to the plough.[55] But when the ass Timer feigns death in front of Malpertuus to help Liétard to pay back the foxes, Hermeline is deceived. She wants to tie Renart and herself with the stolen traps to the ass's body and bring in the food. Renart – who has experience with feigning death – is not deceived, and so refuses. When Hermeline tries to bring in the body by herself and ties herself to a leg of the ass, Timer runs away with her and brings her to Liétard (Figure 15). The peasant tries to kill Hermeline with a sword but succeeds only in severing Timer's leg from his body. Hermeline is now free and returns with the leg to Malpertuus. Renart starts laughing when he sees her coming, but the text does not explain whether that is because he is glad that his wife is still alive, that they have at least some food, or because he thinks the situation is funny. He makes very clear, however, that he, and not she, is going to decide what will happen now. So, this is a case where Hermeline's advice is useful on one occasion and wrong on another. Renart is clever and independent

Figure 15. *Hermeline bound to Timer the ass. Part of a mosaic in the Cathedral of Lescar* (1130–40).

enough to follow the good advice and to ignore the bad. He is clearly the person who should decide.

In branch Ib, Renart is absent from home for a very long time and Hermeline assumes after a while that he is dead.[56] She decides to re-marry with the young badger Poncet. The wedding ceremony is delayed because the new pair cannot find a minstrel for the festivities. Renart comes, disguised as a minstrel, traps Poncet and sees him killed, returns to Malpertuis, abuses Hermeline both verbally and physically and throws her out, together with Hersent, who is there as a sort of bridesmaid. Outside they talk about their situation and Hermeline discovers that Renart has slept with Hersent. She is furious and a row erupts between the two women. Their verbal and physical behaviour (cursing, scratching, hair pulling, etc.) fits all prejudices and stereotypes regarding offended women. A passing priest stops their row and advises them to go back to their husbands and beg for mercy. Hermeline and Renart are reconciled. Renart tells his wife all that happened to him during his absence and she laughs at his tale. Again, it becomes clear that Renart is the dominant partner in the couple. He sees Hermeline as his property. No other male has a right to her. But, in the end, they again live harmoniously; Hermeline in her submissive and supportive role, Renart as the centre of attention.

Hermeline and Reynard have children. They are always boys, but their number differs. In the *Roman de Renart* they have three boys, in *Renart le Contrefait* four and in the Dutch tradition two. In the *Roman de Renart* their role is small. Their hunger is sometimes the starting point of an adventure and they are glad when Renart returns safely. Mostly they are presented as cubs, but in branch Ib they support their mother when she goes to court to pay the ransom for her husband and in branch XI they fight alongside their father, who has made himself emperor, against the army of King Noble. In that branch Hermeline dies from neglect, while Malebranche, one of the sons, dies in a battle. Renart twice shows some sadness, but almost immediately pays attention to something else again. Other things are more important than his love for his family.

We find an extreme example of this attitude in *Renart le Contrefait*.[57] At the beginning of branch V of that text, Renart takes his son Perchehaie with him to get some food. The fox takes his son to a henhouse and instructs him to do exactly as he does himself and then to go his own way. Renart grabs a cock by the neck so that it is unable to make noise. He hides himself in a barn. Perchehaie tries to do the same but

grabs another cock at the back so that it crows in panic. The farmers come and close all possible exits. When Perchehaie tries to escape, he is killed by dogs. Renart sees this from his hiding place and comments on it. It is Perchehaie's own fault because he was so clumsy. Now he must die. Renart will not help him because he does not want to die too. He would sacrifice a thousand sons to stay alive himself; he can always beget new ones. The meaning of this cynical story is not immediately clear, but it seems to contain a double lesson. The first: pay attention to every situation and handle it accordingly, do not follow a fixed pattern. From the moment that Perchehaie's cock started to crow, Renart's example became useless for the young fox. If he had fled immediately, perhaps he would have saved his life. But he tried to follow his father. The second: take care of yourself, because others will not rescue you (Renart had instructed his son to go his own way after the catch). This pessimistic view on relations may be found in other fourteenth-century texts (e.g., in the *Roman de la rose*) but it is unique in the Reynard tradition.

For instance, we see the completely opposite image in the Dutch tradition. There we find three speeches that Reynaert makes about his two sons. When Reynaert goes to court he asks Hermeline to care for their children because he loves them very much.[58] He hopes Reynaerdijn will resemble him when he is grown and he calls Rossel *een scone dief* (l. 1415; literally 'a good thief', metaphorically 'a fine scoundrel'). When he plans to go to court for the second time, he praises them to Grimbeert.[59] They are already good at catching prey, but he wants to teach them to protect themselves from snares, hunters and dogs before he sends them out on their own. (What a difference from the situation in *Renart le Contrefait*!) They resemble Reynaert because they show friendly behaviour to enemies in order to be able to attack them unexpectedly. The third time that Reynaert talks about his children is during his second treasure story. He describes a mirror that he sent to the queen. His children were very unhappy that he gave the mirror away:

> Dien rouwe die mijn twe kinder dreven
> Om dat spiegel, dat was te vele,
> Want sier hem dic myt groten spele
> In plagen te spiegelen ende voor te springen
> Ende zagen hoe hair stcrtgens hingen
> Ende hoe hem hair muulken stont.[60]

> The mourning that my two children made because of the mirror was enormous, because they reflected themselves often in it with great pleasure, and jumped before it and looked how their little tails hung and how their little muzzles stood.

In all three speeches Reynaert shows that he cares for his children and that he is proud of them. The situation is, however, less positive than it looks. Reynaert calls Rossel *dief* which can be interpreted as an endearing term, but literally it means 'thief'. And if Reynaerdijn really is like Reynaert when he is an adult, we have a second liar, murderer, rapist and so on. Reynaert's words to Grimbeert are even clearer about this. He praises his children because they can beguile others so that they can attack them unexpectedly. This is exactly what Reynaert does, and for his enemies this is disastrous. And the mirror? Of course, the image of the jumping fox cubs is moving, but there is no mirror. Reynaert invented the treasure. In the same way he invented his unhappy children. He only wants to emphasise how perfect a servant he is. For the gain of the queen, he is willing to cause his children grief. Isn't that admirable? On the level of the narrative, Reynaert's words to Hermeline and Grimbeert are true and his words to the court are lies, but for an attentive public all his words are false.

CONCLUSION

The medieval tradition of Reynard stories (or, more generally, fox stories) is enormous. It spans the whole of the Middle Ages and contains many, many tales. These show an enormous variety in their aims and literary technique. But whatever the stories do – making their public laugh, criticising society, presenting a bleak picture of reality, and so on – in all of them the fox is presented as a trickster and a deceiver and his most important weapon is his words. He tells his lies so convincingly that they seem nothing but the truth. But do not trust him, ever!

POSTSCRIPT

IN 1953 SIR ISAIAH BERLIN, a Latvian-born British philosopher, published an essay titled *The Hedgehog and the Fox*. This title refers to a statement ascribed to the Greek poet Archilochus (*c*.680–645 BC): 'a fox knows many things, but a hedgehog knows one big thing'. Berlin uses the hedgehog and the fox as images of two types of thinker and writer. The hedgehogs have one big idea that determines all their doings, or they write about one single theme. Examples include Plato, Dante, Hegel and Nietzsche. The foxes do many different things and demonstrate in their writings many different interests. Examples are Aristotle, Shakespeare and Goethe. This essay has become very popular and the title has become shorthand for the contrast between these two types of human being.

This highlights two things. First, the fox already had a cultural significance long before the Middle Ages. The second, our cultural image of the fox differs fundamentally from its medieval image. For Berlin, foxes are positive characters. They represent some of the greatest thinkers and writers of

western civilisation. The medieval fable of the fox and the cat that we have seen (see pp. 86–8) shows a comparable opposition between an animal with one trick and another with many tricks, but in that fable the fox is seen as a vain boaster and a liar and that is typical of the medieval view of the fox, which was on the whole very negative, while our view today is mostly positive.[1] We tend to forget or neglect some elements that were of central importance in the medieval view of the fox. We never stress that he stinks and we no longer link him to the Devil or evil incarnate. Hunting foxes is forbidden by law in many countries because it is no longer seen as the removal of vermin or as a sport but as something cruel and unnecessary. We stress, just as medieval authors did, that foxes have a red pelt and a bushy tail and that they are sly and cunning, but we give these elements a different meaning. Although many modern people are against the wearing of fur, fox pelts are still admired and are often used to create an image of luxury and refinement. The vixen is no longer characterised as malicious but has become a metaphor for a sexually attractive, albeit slightly dangerous woman. And in stories, the fox is no longer a danger to social stability but represents someone who does not want to be hemmed in by social restrictions and who defends his freedom against larger powers by being cleverer than they are.

Our stories about foxes, however, are still based mainly on the medieval tradition. In German-speaking countries Goethe's *Reineke Fuchs*, a descendant of *Reynaerts historie*, is still reprinted and new adaptations appear regularly. In England, there is new interest in Caxton's *History of Reynard the Fox*, another descendant of *Reynaerts historie*.[2] In France, the

Roman de Renart has become popular again since the middle of the nineteenth century, especially in the prose reworking of Paulin Paris (1861). In the Low Countries, *Reynaerts historie* has become almost invisible but *Van den vos Reynaerde* is seen as one of the most, if not *the* most, important literary work ever written in Dutch. Its retellings, reworkings and adaptations are numbered in the hundreds.[3] The changed modern image of the fox, however, has influenced the great majority of these retellings and adaptations. They are based on medieval plots and story lines, but their mentality and their meaning are modern. It is striking how well the medieval material can adapt to changing social convictions and variable aesthetic preferences.

In some parts of Europe these medieval Reynard stories also lead to other phenomena. This is especially visible in the Waasland, a region between Ghent and the modern border between Belgium and the Netherlands. The original text of *Van den vos Reynaerde* contains the names of some places from this region and on that basis the people there have claimed that text as their own. And they honour it by producing Reynaert beer and Reynaert cake, by erecting Reynaert statues and producing Reynaert murals and stained-glass windows, by naming schools and restaurants after him, by periodically producing drama or musical versions of the story and by designing routes for walking, cycling and driving that visit places that have a link with the story.[4] Behind many of these phenomena we glimpse not only cultural but also economic motivations, but it is still striking that it is the Reynaert material and not something else that creates all this activity. This would merit a study of its own, and indeed, there are more subjects that are touched upon in

this book that deserve a more elaborate analysis. It seems as if the *matière renardienne* is inexhaustible. This is not a new idea, but one that had already been formulated in the fourteenth century by the author of *Renart le Contrefait*. Thus, we may end with his words:

> Car sur Regnart poeult on gloser,
> Penser, estudïer, muser,
> Plus que sur toete rien qui soit.[5]

For one can write commentaries on Reynard, think about him, study him, muse about him, more than on anything else that exists.

APPENDIX

Here, follow the medieval Reynard stories in chronological order. Details regarding the manuscripts, editions, translations and the research on each text may be found via *https://www.arlima.net/* (last accessed 20 May 2022).

Text	Date	Localisation
Ysengrimus	1148–9	Ghent
Roman de Renart	Begins 1174–7	Unclear
	First ms collections *c.*1200	Suggestions of Northern France and Flanders
	Ends before 1250	
Reinhart Fuchs	*c.*1200	Alsace
Rainaldo e Lesengrino	Begins thirteenth century	Italy
Philippe de Novarre, 'Branche'	First half of the thirteenth century	Cyprus
Ménestrel de Reims, 'Récit'	*c.*1260	Reims/Northern France/Flanders

Text	Date	Localisation
Van den vos Reynaerde	Middle of the thirteenth century (before 1279)	Ghent
Ruteboef, Renart le Bestourné	c.1261	Paris/Champagne
Le Couronnement de Renart	1263–70	Flanders
Reinardus Vulpes	c.1275	Bruges
Jacquemart Gielée, Renart le Nouvel	Before 1288	Lille
The Vox and the Wolf	Thirteenth century	Southern England
Renart le Contrefait	First red. 1319–23 Second red. 1328–48	Author is from Troyes Mss from Northern France
Chaucer, Nun's Priest Tale	Between 1387 and 1400	London
Reynaerts historie	1373–c.1470 Probably fifteenth century	Ypres
Jean Tenessax, Livre de Maistre Renart	1466	Northern France?

ENDNOTES

INTRODUCTION

1. Martin Wallen, *Fox* (London: Reaktion Books, 2006). See also *https://animaldiversity.org/accounts/Vulpes_vulpes/* (last accessed 19 May 2022). For the medieval ideas about the eating habits of foxes, see p. 68

2. Kerstin Rodin, *Räven predikar för Gässen. En studie av ett ordspråk i senmedeltida ikonografi* (Stockholm: Almqvist and Wiksell, 1983).

3. Based on Kristopher Poole, 'Foxes and Badgers in Anglo-Saxon Life and Landscape', *Archeological Journal*, 172(2) (2015), 389–422.

4. For the post-medieval fox hunt as amusement, see Wallen, *Fox*, pp. 91–120.

5. See Edward of York, *Master of Game* and, for example, Vincent of Beauvais, *Speculum naturale*, book 19, chapter 123. Cf. my Chapter 3, notes 24 and 15 respectively.

6. Based on Rolf Roosen, '"Fuchshoden machet diejenigen hurtig, so sich der Weiber nicht gebrauchen können." Der Rotfuchs, ein Parforceritt durch Bibel, Tierepos und Fachliteratur', *Log. Zeitschrift für internationale Literatur*, 53 (2010), 175–88. Pamela H. Smith, 'Making as Knowing: Craft as Natural Philosophy', in Pamela H. Smith, Amy R. W. Meyers and Harold Cook (eds),

Ways of Making and Knowing (Ann Arbor MI: University of Michigan Press, 2014), pp. 17–47, esp. p. 31.

7. Based on Elspeth M. Veale, *The English Fur Trade in the Later Middle Ages* (London, 1953; reprint Oxford, New York: Oxford University Press, 1966) and Robert Delort, *Le commerce des fourrures en occident à la fin du moyen âge (vers 1300–vers 1450)*, 2 vols (Rome: École Française de Rome, 1978). The website *http://cottesimple.com/articles/fur-primer/* (last accessed 21 May 2022) offers excellent information in text and image about fur as decoration of clothes.

8. Based on Delort, *Le commerce des fourrures*, pp. 947, 968, 712 respectively.

9. Based on Delort, *Le commerce des fourrures*, pp. 717 and 166, 703, 548 respectively.

10. When writing about a specific text, I will use the language specific form of the name, but in general remarks I use always the English form, Reynard.

11. John Cummins, *The Hound and the Hawk: the Art of Medieval Hunting* (London: Phoenix Press, 1988), pp. 144–6.

12. Based on Nancy Freeman Regalado, 'Tristan and Renart. Two Tricksters', *L'Esprit créateur*, 16 (1976), 30–8. Jean Batany, *Scène et coulisses du 'Roman de Renart'* (Paris: Sedes, 1989), pp. 23–45. Alison Williams, *Tricksters and Pranksters: Roguery in French and German Literature of the Middle Ages and the Renaissance* (Amsterdam and Atlanta GA: Rodopi, 2000).

13. For the diverse meanings of 'trickster', see Batany, *Scène et coulisses du 'Roman de Renart'*, pp. 25–7.

14. An excellent introduction to the study of images and the relations between images and texts is Kenneth Varty, *Reynard, Renart, Reinaert, and Other Foxes in Medieval England: the Iconographic Evidence* (Amsterdam: Amsterdam University Press, 1999). An annotated bibliography of the iconographical research of the past fifty years may be found in Kenneth Varty and Paul Wackers,

'A Selective Survey of Visual Representations of Reynardian Literature and Fox Lore in the Last Fifty Years', *Reinardus*, 30 (2018), 212–58, esp. 245–57.

15. Based on Kenneth Varty, 'La mosaïque de Lescar et la datation des contes de Renart le goupil', in Kenneth Varty (ed.), *À la recherche du Roman de Renart*, 2 vols (New Alyth: Lochee Publications, 1991), II, pp. 318–29.

16. A brilliant analysis of the beast literature in Britain is Jill Mann, *From Aesop to Reynard: Beast Literature in Medieval Britain* (Oxford: Oxford University Press, 2009). For fox stories, see Chapter 6 and use the index.

17. The best guide to texts and images regarding the fox from the British isles is Varty, *Reynard, Renart, Reinaert, and Other Foxes in Medieval England*.

18. See Kenneth Varty, 'Les Funérailles de Renart le goupil', in Varty, *À la recherche du Roman de Renart*, II, pp. 361–90. Publications on this theme in less accessible languages but with excellent illustrations are *www.isolainvisibile.it/Arte/Il%20Pavimento%20 Musivo%20di%20San%20Donato/IlFuneraleDellaVolpe.html* (last accessed 19 May 2022); and Jos Houtsma, 'Zeven Italiaanse vossen', *Tiecelijn*, 33, Jaarboek 13 (2020), 237–44.

19. For a thorough analysis of this scene and its context, see Jean R. Scheidegger, 'Renart et Arthur à la cathédrale de Modène', in Varty, *À la recherche du Roman de Renart*, II, pp. 391–414.

20. Cf. Rodin, *Räven predikar för Gässen* and Varty, *Reynard, Renart, Reinaert, and Other Foxes in Medieval England*, pp. 131–62.

21. Based on Varty, *Reynard, Renart, Reinaert, and Other Foxes in Medieval England*, pp. 31–54.

22. A fox bearing off with a goose seems unnatural but it is possible that the image of a fox with a goose flung over his back was based on observation of natural foxes, because medieval geese were far smaller than modern ones and wild geese are smaller than tame ones.

23. See Kenneth Varty, *Reynard the Fox: a Study of the Fox in Medieval English Art* (Leicester: Leicester University Press, 1967), pp. 26–7 and Ill. 11. For other examples of the fox as bad 'contra-image', see Varty, *Reynard, Renart, Reinaert, and Other Foxes in Medieval England*, pp. 156–7.

24. Varty, *Reynard, Renart, Reinaert, and Other Foxes in Medieval England*, pp. 118–24.

25. Varty, *Reynard, Renart, Reinaert, and Other Foxes in Medieval England*, pp. 60–1.

1. THE FOX AND MEDIEVAL RELIGION

1. This section is mainly based on P. W. M. Wackers, *De waarheid als leugen. Een interpretatie van Reynaerts historie* (Utrecht: HES, 1986), pp. 55–66.

2. All quotations (in Latin or in English) from the Bible or references to it are based on *www.Biblegateway.com* (accessed 19 May 2022). I use the Douai-Rheims translation of the Vulgate.

3. For more on this see Frans van Liere, *An Introduction to the Medieval Bible* (Cambridge: Cambridge University Press, 2014), pp. 116–23. Many medieval exegetes discern three levels in the spiritual meaning: allegory – what you should believe; moral sense – what you should do; anagogy – what you should strive for (pp. 120–3). For the interpretation of the fox this division is unimportant. I use the term 'allegorical interpretation' not in this specific, technical way but to indicate a metaphorical interpretation that is based on the divine world order.

4. Eligius Dekkers and Iohannes Fraipont (eds), *Sancti Avrelii Avgvstini Enarrationes in Psalmos. LI–C* (Turnhout: Brepols, 1956), p. 1128 (in Ps. 80:14).

5. J. P. Migne, *Patrologiae Cursus Completus. Series Latina*, vol. 113 (Paris: Garnier, 1852), p. 1141.

6. J. Leclercq, C. H. Talbot and H. M. Rochais (eds), *Sermones super cantica canticorum*, 36–86 (Rome: Editiones cistercienses, 1958).

7. C. Hap (ed.), 'Een 14e-eeuws Middelnederlands berijmd commentaar op het Hooglied. Kritische studie en uitgave van de tekst' (unpublished PhD thesis, Université catholique de Louvain, 1975), *www.dbnl.org/tekst/_com006comm02_01/index.php* (last accessed 19 May 2022).

8. Hap, 'Een 14e-eeuws Middelnederlands berijmd commentaar', caput 128. The same ideas are repeated in a more abstract way in cap. 130.

9. For details see Wackers, *De waarheid als leugen*, pp. 64–5.

10. *De Universo* VIII, 1, cited via Marion Darilek, *Füchsische Desintegration. Studien zum Reinhart Fuchs im Vergleich zum Roman de Renart* (Heidelberg: Universitätsverlag Winter, 2020), pp. 285–6.

11. Based on Dominic Alexander, *Saints and Animals in the Middle Ages* (Woodbridge: The Boydell Press, 2008), pp. 71–2; and Niall Mac Coitir, *Ireland's Animals* (Cork: The Collins Press: 2010, 2nd edn 2015), chapter Fox. All the cases I have found, concern Irish saints. I do not know whether this is significant.

12. Based on Kenneth Varty, *Reynard, Renart, Reinaert, and Other Foxes in Medieval England: The Iconographic Evidence* (Amsterdam: Amsterdam University Press, 1999), pp. 55–86. Kerstin Rodin, *Räven predikar för Gässen. En studie av ett ordspråk i senmedeltida ikonografi* (Stockholm: Almqvist and Wiksell, 1983).

13. Varty, *Reynard, Renart, Reinaert*, p. 59. For more information on the Reynard texts mentioned here and in the following, see *www.arlima.net* (last accessed 19 May 2022).

14. Based on Nancy Freeman Regalado, 'Staging the *Roman de Renart*: Medieval Theater and the Diffusion of Political Concerns into Popular Culture', *Mediaevalia*, 18 (1995), 111–41. Varty, *Reynard, Renart, Reinaert*, pp. 84–5.

15. See the English translation in Regalado, 'Staging the *Roman de Renart*', 136.

16. See Varty, *Reynard, Renart, Reinaert*, pp. 79–84 on the images.

17. Jill Mann (ed. and trans.), *Ysengrimus* (Cambridge MA and London: Harvard University Press, 2013), pp. 216–73, book 4, ll. 1–810.

18. D. D. R. Owen, *The Romance of Reynard the Fox* (Oxford and New York: Oxford University Press, 1994), pp. 140–6. On the name 'branch' for a separate story within a larger corpus, see pp. 92–3.

19. Owen, *The Romance of Reynard the Fox*, p. 146.

20. André Bouwman and Bart Besamusca (eds), *Of Reynaert the Fox: text and facing translation of the Middle Dutch beast epic 'Van den vos Reynaerde'*; edited with an introduction, notes and glossary and translated by Thea Summerfield; includes a chapter on Middle Dutch by Matthias Hüning and Ulrike Vogl (Amsterdam: Amsterdam University Press, 2009), pp. 218–21, ll. 3016–28.

2. THE FOX AND MEDIEVAL SCHOLARSHIP

1. Based on Willene B. Clark, *A Medieval Book of Beasts: The Second-family Bestiary: Commentary, Art, Text and Translation* (Woodbridge: The Boydell Press, 2006) and Elisabeth Morrison and Larissa Grollemond (eds), *Book of Beasts: The Bestiary in the Medieval World* (Los Angeles CA: J. Paul Getty Museum, 2019). The latter book also provides information on the influence of the bestiaries in medieval culture. Regarding images, see Kenneth Varty, *Reynard, Renart, Reinaert, and Other Foxes in Medieval England: The Iconographic Evidence* (Amsterdam: Amsterdam University Press, 1999), pp. 171–7. Kenneth Varty, 'Playing Dead: the Bestiary Fox on Misericords and in the *Roman de Renart*', in *The Playful Middle Ages: Meanings of Play and Plays of Meaning: Essays in Memory of Elaine C. Block*, ed. Paul Hardwick (Turnhout: Brepols, 2010), pp. 233–44. The bestiary website of David Badke is also very useful. See *www.bestiary.ca* (last accessed 18 May 2022).

2. For more details, see Clark, *The Book of Beasts*, pp. 9–10.

3. More about the tradition in Clark, *The Book of Beasts*, pp. 7–20; and Morrison and Grollemond, *Book of Beasts*, pp. 31–8, 88–174.

4. Clark, A *Medieval Book of Beasts*, pp. 141–2, chapter 25. |*Intrabun* is in the Vulgate: *Introibunt.*|

5. Stills from this film are reproduced in Varty, *Reynard, Renart, Reinaert*, pp. 173–4.

6. Gabriel Bianciotto (ed.), *Bestiaires du Moyen Age* (Paris: Stock, 1980), p. 38.

7. Bianciotto, *Bestiaires du Moyen Age*, pp. 91–2.

8. Gerd Dicke and Klaus Grubmüller, *Die Fabeln des Mittelalters und der frühen Neuzeit. Ein Katalog der deutschen Versionen und ihrer lateinischen Entsprechungen* (München: Wilhelm Fink Verlag, 1987), pp. 243–4 (nr. 206). P. W. M. Wackers, *De waarheid als leugen, een interpretatie van Reynaerts historie* (Utrecht: HES, 1986), pp. 101–2.

9. For a longer description, see Kenneth Varty, *Reynard the Fox: A Study of the Fox in Medieval English Art* (Leicester: Leicester University Press, 1967), pp. 83–6. For an overview of the full influence of the bestiary fox on the *Roman de Renart*, see Kenneth Varty, 'Le goupil des bestiaires dans le Roman de Renart', in Kenneth Varty, À *la recherche du Roman de Renart*, 2 vols (New Alyth: Lochee Publications, 1991), II, pp. 344–60.

10. Paul Wackers (ed.), *Reynaert in tweevoud: Deel II. Reynaerts historie* (Amsterdam: Bert Bakker, 2002), pp. 163–6, ll. 3558–617; p. 199, ll. 4485–507.

11. Based on Jeanette Beer, 'Clergie? Chevalerie? Renardie? *Le Bestiaire d'amour* and a Woman's Response', in Adrian P. Tudor and Alan Hindley (eds), *Grant Risee? The Medieval Comic Presence. La Présence comique médiévale: Essays in Memory of Brian J. Levy* (Turnhout: Brepols, 2006), pp. 337–46.

12. Quotation and translation both taken from Beer, 'Clergie? Chevalerie? Renardie?', p. 345.

13. Beer, 'Clergie? Chevalerie? Renardie?', p. 345.

14. For more information about medieval encyclopaedias as a phenomenon, see Peter Binkley (ed.), *Pre-Modern Encyclopaedic Texts: Proceedings of the Second COMERS Congress, Groningen,*

1–4 July 1996 (Leiden: Brill, 1997). Christel Meier, 'Tendenzen der neueren Forschung zur Enzyklopädie des Mittelalters, in Amand Berteloot and Dieter Hellfaier (eds), *Jacob van Maerlants 'Der naturen bloeme' und das Umfeld. Vorläufer – Redaktionen – Rezeption* (Münster: Waxmann, 2001), pp. 29–47. Joëlle Ducos (ed.), *Encyclopédie médiévale et langues européennes: Réception et diffusion du De proprietatibus rerum de Barthélemy l'Anglais dans les langues vernaculaires* (Paris: Honoré Champion, 2014). Cf. also Emily Steiner, 'Encyclopedic Beasts', in Morrison and Grollemond, *Book of Beasts*, pp. 237–44.

15. *The Etymologies of Isidore of Seville*, ed. and trans. Stephen A. Barney, W. J. Lewis, J. A. Beach and Oliver Berhof, in collaboration with Muriel Hall (Cambridge: Cambridge University Press, 2006), see XII, ii, 29. Hrabanus Maurus, *De universo*, VIII, 1, see Marion Darilek, *Füchsische Desintegration. Studien zum Reinhart Fuchs im Vergleich zum Roman de Renart* (Heidelberg: Universitätsverlag Winter, 2020), pp. 285–6. Alexander Neckam, *De naturis rerum libri duo* … ed. Thomas Wright (London: Longman, Roberts and Green, 1863). See Cap. CXXV–CXXVII, pp. 204–7. Thomas Cantimpratensis, *Liber de natura rerum, Teil I: Text*, ed. H. Boese (Berlin and New York: De Gruyter, 1973). See book 4, cap. 108. Bartholomaeus Anglicus, *De proprietatibus rerum*. Frankfurt 1601 (Photographic reprint: Frankfurt am Main: Minerva, 1964). See book 18, cap. 112. Vincent of Beauvais, *Speculum naturale*, version Douai 1624, *http://sourcencyme.irht.cnrs.fr/encyclopedie/speculum_naturale_version_sm_trifaria_ed_douai_1624* (last accessed 19 May 2022). See book 19, cap. 121–3. Albertus Magnus, *De animalibus libri XXVI*, ed. Hermann Stadler, *Vol.* II (*Buch XIII–XXVI*) (Münster: Asschendorffsche Verlagsbuchhandlung, 1920). See liber XXII, tract. 2, cap. 1, 110, pp. 1427–8.

16. On Aristotle's ideas about the fox, see Wallen, *Fox*, pp. 8–12. The ideas that are handed down include the notion that the penis of the fox is bony, that the young are born incompletely formed,

and that the raven and the fox are friends. Aristotle states that
the vixen licks her young into form. (Medieval bestiaries say this
about the bear.) In medieval encyclopaedias it is said only that
the young foxes are born blind. That the raven and the fox are
friends is sometimes changed into the hart and the fox being
friends, probably because of a misunderstanding somewhere
in the tradition. All these elements are found only in the
encyclopaedic tradition, nowhere else.

17. *Etymologiae* XII, ii, 29. Translation by Barney e.a. (cf. note 15).

18. Bohdana Librová, 'Le renard dans le *cubiculum taxi*: les avatars
    d'un exemplum et le symbolisme du blaireau', *Le Moyen Âge*, 109
    (2003), 79–111, esp. 107–8.

19. Modern biologists observed this behaviour. See Librova, 'Le
    renard dans le *cubiculum taxi*', 108, but cf. also 94.

20. I have used scans from the edition *Reductorii moralis* Petri
    Berchorii … (Venice: Hieronymus Scotus, 1575): *https://archive.org/
    details/bub_gb_cu*DYTC-VfM8C/*page/n3/mode/2up* (last accessed
    19 May 2022). See Liber X, cap. 110, pp. 445–6.

21. Librová, 'Le renard dans le *cubiculum taxi*', 92–3. She gives also
    examples of a wider use of the first interpretation, see 85–92.

22. Based on David Dalby, *Lexicon of the Medieval German Hunt* (Berlin:
    De Gruyter, 1965); John Cummins, *The Hound and the Hawk: the Art
    of Medieval Hunting* (London: Phoenix Press, 1988); and An Smets
    and Baudouin van den Abeele, 'Medieval Hunting', in Birgitte
    Resl, *A Cultural History of Animals in the Medieval Age* (Oxford and
    New York: Berg, 2007; reprint 2011), pp. 59–79.

23. For an overview of the tradition see Smets and Van den Abeele,
    'Medieval Hunting', pp. 65–71.

24. I use the following editions: Gunnar Tilander (ed.), *Les livres du
    roy Modus et de la royne Ratio*, publiés avec introduction, notes et
    glossaire par, 2 vols (Paris: Société des anciens textes français,
    1932). See pp. 89–92 (chapter 52) and pp. 151–2 (chapter 79).
    Gunnar Tilander (ed.), Gaston Phébus, *Livre de chasse*, édité

avec introduction, glossaire et reproduction des 87 miniatures du manuscrit 616 de la Bibliothèque nationale de Paris par – (Karlshamn: Johansson, 1971; reprint: 1976; Graz: Akad. Druckund Verlagsanstalt, 1994). See pp. 99–101 (chapter 11) and pp. 242–5 (chapter 56). William A. and Florence Baillie-Grohman (eds), *The Master of Game, by Edward, Second Duke of York. The Oldest English Book of Hunting*, 2nd edn (London: Chatto and Windus, 1909). See pp. 64–7 (Chapter 8) and pp. 212–4. Websites with scans of a manuscript of the *Livre de chasse* are: *https://gallica.bnf.fr/ark:/12148/btv1b52505055c/f1.item* and *www.themorgan.org/collection/Illuminating-the-Medieval-Hunt/thumbs* (last accessed 19 May 2022).

25. The detail that foxes prefer young geese makes it more probable that the images of a fox running off with a goose slung on his back are based on observation. Cf. pp. 16–17.

26. An example of the fox as scavenger from Irish poetry are these lines from a poem describing the ruin of Swords, formerly a place of learning: 'I am off to Swords again.' / 'How are things shaping there?' / 'Oh, things are keeping fair; / Foxes round churchyards bare / Gnawing the guts of men.' David Greene and Frank O'Connor (eds), *A Golden Treasury of Irish Poetry* AD 600–1200 (London: Macmillan, 1967), p. 11. The idea of the fox as scavenger also led to the idea of the *sinnach brothlaig(e)* ('the fox of the kitchen'), a term for the poorest of beggars who were allowed to steal scraps of food from the kitchen (personal communication by Peter Schrijver, chair for Celtic Studies, Utrecht University; cf. Niall Mac Coitir, *Ireland's Animals*, 2nd edn (Cork: The Collins Press, 2015), 'Fox'). An example from German literature are the lines 5042–44 of the *Alexander* of Pfaffe Lambrecht, which describe what happened after a battle: 'fôchse dar ouh quâmen / grôze ûzir mâzen / Di lîchamen si âzen' ('very large foxes came there; they ate the corpses'). Cited from Karl Kinzel (ed.) *Lamprechts Alexander* (Halle a. S.: Buchhandlung des Waisenhauses, 1884).

27. On *par force* hunting see Cummins, *The Hound and the Hawk*, pp. 15 and 32–46. For the development of the modern fox hunt Wallen, *Fox*, pp. 91–120.

28. Quotation from Varty, *Reynard the Fox*, p. 25, being a fairly precise translation of *Les Livres du roy Modus et de la royne Ratio*, ed. Tilander, p. 90 l. 6 – p. 91 l. 45. I have changed Varty's use of the word 'fagott'.

29. Large quotations from a translation of and commentary on this fox hunt may be found in Cummins, *The Hound and the Hawk*, pp. 144–6.

30. Cummins, *The Hound and the Hawk*, p. 146.

31. Cummins, *The Hound and the Hawk*, p. 143.

32. Dalby, *Lexicon of the Medieval German Hunt*, pp. xiii and 84–5.

33. Short reference in Cummins, *The Hound and the Hawk*, p. 142. For a more elaborate discussion, see Marcelle Thiébaux, 'Sir Gawain, the Fox Hunt, and Henry of Lancaster', *Neuphilologische Mitteilungen*, 71 (1970), 469–79.

34. See *Les livres du roy Modus et de la royne Ratio*, ed. Tilander, pp. 151–2 (Chapter 79).

3.   THE FOX AND MEDIEVAL LITERATURE

1. For an overview of the tradition and a guide to further research, see Jill Mann, *From Aesop to Reynard: Beast Literature in Medieval Britain* (Oxford: Oxford University Press, 2009), pp. 2–16.

2. Gerd Dicke and Klaus Grubmüller, *Die Fabeln des Mittelalters und der frühen Neuzeit. Ein Katalog der deutschen Versionen und ihrer lateinischen Entsprechungen* (München: Wilhelm Fink Verlag, 1987).

3. For more information see Ulrike Bodemann, 'Speculum sapientiae', in *Verfasserlexikon. Die deutsche Literatur des Mittelalters*, ed. Kurt Ruh *e.a.*, vol. 9 (Berlin: Walter de Gruyter, 2012), pp. 65–7. The only existing edition is Johann Georg Theodor Grässe (ed.), *Die beiden ältesten lateinischen Fabelbücher des Mittelalters. Des Bisschofs Cyrillus Speculum sapientiae und des Nicolaus Pergamenus*

Dialogus creaturarum (Tübingen: Bibliothek des Litterarischen Vereins in Stuttgart, 1880), pp. 1–124. Cf., *https://archive.org/details/b21782076/page/n5/mode/2up* (last accessed 20 May 2022).

4.   Based on Paul Wackers, 'The Image of the Fox in Middle Dutch Literature', *The Fox and Other Animals: Reinardus*, Special Volume (1993), 181–98, esp. note 38. This article inspired much of what is written here about fables.

5.   Cf. Dicke and Grubmüller, *Die Fabeln*, nr. 171 and 201.

6.   Book 2, fable 15, Grässe, *Die beiden ältesten lateinischen Fabelbücher*, pp. 51–2. Cf. Dicke and Grubmüller, *Die Fabeln*, nr. 187.

7.   Book 1 fable 5, Grässe, *Die beiden ältesten lateinischen Fabelbücher*, pp. 9–10. Cf. Dicke and Grubmüller, Die Fabeln, nr. 206.

8.   Cf. Dicke and Grubmüller, *Die Fabeln*, nr. 212.

9.   Cf. Dicke and Grubmüller, *Die Fabeln*, nr. 214.

10.   Cf. Dicke and Grubmüller, *Die Fabeln*, nr. 174.

11.   Based on Mann, *From Aesop to Reynard*, pp. 53–76 and Harriet Spiegel (ed. and trans.), *Marie de France, Fables* (Toronto, Buffalo and London: University of Toronto Press: 1987).

12.   Spiegel, *Marie de France, Fables*, pp. 226–7.

13.   Spiegel's translation.

14.   Based on Spiegel, *Marie de France, Fables*, pp. 228–9. Mann, *From Aesop to Reynard*, pp. 67–72. Cf. Dicke and Grubmüller, *Die Fabeln*, nr. 196.

15.   Mann, *From Aesop to Reynard*, pp. 14–6.

16.   See also John C. Jacobs (ed.), *The Fables of Odo of Cheriton* (Syracuse NY: Syracuse University Press, 1985).

17.   Léopold Hervieux, *Les fabulistes latins depuis le siècle d'Auguste jusqu'à la fin du Moyen Age*, vol. IV, photographic reprint (Hildesheim and New York: Olms, 1970), pp. 212–13.

18.   Hervieux, *Les fabulistes latins*, IV, pp. 381–3.

19.   Hervieux, *Les fabulistes latins*, IV, p. 383.

20.   My overview here is selective but all texts from the tradition are listed in the Appendix. Information about the manuscripts,

editions, translations and studies of a specific text may be found
via *www.arlima.net* (last accessed 20 May 2022). Informative short
overviews are Marc-René Jung, 'Epische Formen in Frankreich.
Der "Roman de Renart"', in *Neues Handbuch der Literaturwissenschaft*,
vol. 7, Henning Krauβ (ed.), *Europäisches Hochmittelalter*
(Wiesbaden: Akademische Verlagsgesellschaft Athenaion, 1981),
pp. 413–21, 423–4. Paul Wackers, 'Reynard the Fox', in Willem
P. Gerritsen and Anthony G. van Melle (eds), *A Dictionary of
Medieval Heroes: Characters in Medieval Narrative Traditions and Their
Afterlife in Literature, Theatre and the Visual Arts*, trans. Tanis Guest
(Woodbridge: The Boydell Press, 1998), pp. 211–19. A book that
discusses the main texts from the tradition and gives useful
summaries of them is Thomas W. Best, *Reynard the Fox* (Boston:
Twayne Publishers, 1983). For its weaknesses, see *Speculum*, 59
(1984), 621–3.

21. On the *Ysengrimus* and the preceding Latin tradition see Jan
Ziolkowski, *Talking Animals: Medieval Latin Beast Poetry, 750–1150*
(Philadelphia PA: University of Pennsylvania Press, 1993). On the
necessary adaptations to change a short story into a beast epic,
see esp. pp. 198–210.

22. Ziolkowski, *Talking Animals*, pp. 63–6.

23. Ziolkowski, *Talking Animals*, pp. 153–97. The *Ecbasis captivi* is often
discussed together with the *Ysengrimus* because the central part
of that text resembles the *Ysengrimus* in many aspects. However,
in the *Ecbasis* the animals do not yet have names. Its central part
tells about the conflict between a wolf and a fox.

24. Ziolkowski, *Talking Animals*, pp. 48–54.

25. Kenneth Varty, *Reynard, Renart, Reinaert, and Other Foxes in Medieval
England: The Iconographic Evidence* (Amsterdam: Amsterdam
University Press, 1999), pp. 31–6. Mann, *From Aesop to Reynard*,
pp. 238–61.

26. On the French Renart stories and their offspring see John Flinn,
Le Roman de Renart dans la littérature française et dans les littératures

étrangères au Moyen Age (Paris: Presses Universitaires de France, 1963). A guide to research on this text corpus is Kenneth Varty, *The Roman de Renart: A Guide to Scholarly Work* (Lanham MD and London: The Scarecrow Press, 1998). There are many editions of the original together with a French translation. I have used Armand Strubel and others (eds), *Le Roman de Renart* (Paris: Gallimard, 1998). A good English translation is D. D. R. Owen, *The Romance of Reynard the Fox* (Oxford and New York: Oxford University Press, 1994). Cf., *https://archive.org/details/romanceofreynard00* (last accessed 19 May 2022).

27. The chronology of the branches was determined by Lucien Foulet, *Le Roman de Renart* (Paris: Champion, 1914; several reprints).

28. For the names and the numbering of the branches and their distribution over the manuscripts see Varty, *The Roman de Renart: A Guide to Scholarly Work*, pp. 1–7.

29. Elina Suomela-Härmä, *Les structures narratives dans le Roman de Renart* (Helsinki: Suomalainen Tiedeakatemia, 1981).

30. Owen, *The Romance of Reynard the Fox*, pp. 68, 70–1.

31. For an edition with English translation see André Bouwman and Bart Besamusca (eds), *Of Reynaert the Fox: text and facing translation of the Middle Dutch beast epic 'Van den vos Reynaerde'*, edited with an introduction, notes and glossary and translated by Thea Summerfield; includes a chapter on Middle Dutch by Matthias Hüning and Ulrike Vogl (Amsterdam: Amsterdam University Press, 2009).

32. Bouwman and Besamusca, *Of Reynaert the Fox*, pp. 34–5.

33. Cf. Paul Wackers (ed.), *Reynaert in tweevoud: Deel II. Reynaerts historie* (Amsterdam: Bert Bakker, 2002), p. 325 rr. 7785–91 and pp. 327–8.

34. See on the Leeu books Paul Wackers, 'The Printed Dutch Reynaert Tradition: From the Fifteenth to the Nineteenth Century', in Kenneth Varty (ed.), *Reynard the Fox: Social*

Engagement and Cultural Metamorphoses in the Beast Epic from the Middle Ages to the Present (New York and Oxford: Berghahn, 2000), pp. 73–103.

35. For a bibliographical overview of this tradition, see Hubertus Menke, *Bibliotheca Reinardiana. Teil I: Die europäischen Reineke-Fuchs-Drucke bis zum Jahre* 1800 (Stuttgart: Hauswedel & Co., 1992).

36. Much has been written about this motif. As guides to other research, I refer to Kenneth Varty, 'The Fox and the Wolf in the Well: the Metamorphoses of a Comic Motif', in Varty, *Reynard the Fox: Social Engagement and Cultural Metamorphoses in the Beast Epic from the Middle Ages to the present*, pp. 245–56. Mann, *From Aesop to Reynard*, pp. 229–38. Cf. also Dicke and Grubmüller, *Die Fabeln*, nr. 223.

37. More elaborate summaries in Varty, 'The Fox and the Wolf in the Well', pp. 247–8. My text is based on these pages.

38. The Talmud is, after the Bible, the most important book in Judaism. It contains Bible commentaries and guidelines for living correctly.

39. For editions of these texts see Strubel e.a., *Le Roman de Renart*, pp. 163–77 and 1013–37. J. A. W. Bennett and G. V. Smithers (eds), *Early Middle English Verse and Prose* (Oxford: Clarendon Press, 1966; 2nd edn, 1968), pp. 65–76. I discuss only the most frequent of the two *Roman de Renart* versions (pp. 163–77).

40. Strubel e.a., *Le Roman de Renart*, p. 163, ll. 1–7.

41. Owen, *The Romance of Reynard the Fox*, p. 81.

42. Strubel e.a., *Le Roman de Renart*, pp. 170–1, ll. 293–300.

43. Owen, *The Romance of Reynard the Fox*, p. 84.

44. Strubel e.a., *Le Roman de Renart*, p. 174, ll. 431–4.

45. Owen, *The Romance of Reynard the Fox*, pp. 85–6.

46. Cf. Mann, *From Aesop to Reynard*, pp. 237–8.

47. Mann, *From Aesop to Reynard*, pp. 230–1. Jacobs, *The Fables of Odo of Cheriton*, p. 89.

48. George D. Gopen (ed.), *Robert Henryson, Moral Fables* (Notre Dame IN: University of Notre Dame Press, 1987), pp. 156–67.

For background see also Mann, *From Aesop to Reynard*,
pp. 262–305.

49. Gaston Raynaud and Henri Lemaître (eds), *Le Roman de Renart le
Contrefait* (Genève: Slatkine, 1975; reprint of the edn Paris 1914),
II, pp. 55–61, ll. 27787–8380.

50. Karl-Heinz Göttert (ed. and trans.), Heinrich der Glîchezâre,
Reinhart Fuchs. Mittelhochdeutsch / Neuhochdeutsch (Stuttgart: Reclam,
1976), pp. 58–73, ll. 832–1004.

51. Wackers (ed.), *Reynaert in tweevoud*, II, pp. 272–3, ll. 6406–45.

52. We find this first in the *Roman de Renart* (Hersent: branch II–Va;
Fière: branches Ia, XI). In the German and Dutch fox stories we
also find the sex with Hersent. In *Renart le Nouvel* the rape of the
queen (there called Harouge) is retold.

53. Cf. Alison Williams, 'Courtly Lady, Starving Spouse and Partner
in Crime: the Shifting Roles of Hermeline in the Roman de
Renart', *Nottingham French Studies*, 46 (2007), 1–16, esp. 10.

54. The part on Hermeline is based on Roger Bellon, 'Une creation
originale: la fame Renart ou le personage d'Hermeline dans
le *Roman de Renart*', *Reinardus*, Special volume (1993), 13–29.
Williams, 'Courtly Lady'.

55. Owen, *The Romance of Reynard the Fox*, pp. 167–73.

56. Owen, *The Romance of Reynard the Fox*, pp. 45–52.

57. Based on Richard Trachsler, 'Renart als "Demiourgos". Tierfabel
und Weltordnung im "Renart le Contrefait"', in Kathrin
Lukaschek, Michael Waltenberger and Maximilian Wick (eds), *Die
Zeit der sprachbegabten Tiere. Ordnung, Varianz und Geschichtlichkeit (in)
der Tierepik, Beiträge zur mediävistischen Erzählforschung*, Themenheft
11 (2022), 225–52. *https://ojs.uni-oldenburg.de/ojs/index.php/bme/issue/
view/*19 (accessed 14 November 2022).

58. Bouwman and Besamusca, *Of Reynard the Fox*, pp. 124–5, ll.
1407–17; Wackers, *Reynaert in tweevoud*, II, pp. 78–9, ll. 1449–63.

59. Wackers, *Reynaert in tweevoud*, II, pp. 176–7, ll. 3880–906.

60. Wackers, *Reynaert in tweevoud*, II, pp. 252–3, ll. 5893–8.

POSTSCRIPT

1. More on this modern view in Martin Wallen, *Fox* (London: Reaktion Books, 2006), pp. 121–69.
2. See, for instance, James Simpson, *Reynard the Fox: A New Translation* (New York and London: Liveright Publishing Corporation, 2015); and Anne Louise Avery, *Reynard the Fox* (Oxford: Bodleain Library, 2020).
3. See this bibliography, *www.dbnl.org/tekst/_tie002200401_01/_ tie002200401_01_0021.php* (last accessed 20 May 2022).
4. Cf. *www.reynaertgenootschap.be* (last accessed 20 May 2022).
5. Gaston Raynaud and Henri Lemaître (eds), *Le Roman de Renart le Contrefait* (Genève: Slatkine, 1975; reprint of the Paris edn 1914), I, p. 2. These lines are often quoted by modern scholars, so my end is twice unoriginal … but still fitting.

FURTHER READING

THERE IS NO LEADING authority on the medieval fox. The best strategy for further reading will often be consulting the studies mentioned in the notes. The following three books, however, are good, general guides to the study of animal texts, the iconography of the medieval fox and a general cultural approach to the fox.

Mann, Jill, *From Aesop to Reynard: Beast Literature in Medieval Britain* (Oxford: Oxford University Press, 2009). Large parts of this book relate to animals other than the fox, but it is recommended because it describes what animals mean (pp. 28–52) and offers an overview of the whole tradition of animal stories with excellent references.

Varty, Kenneth, *Reynard, Renart, Reinaert, and Other Foxes in Medieval England: The Iconographic Evidence* (Amsterdam: Amsterdam University Press, 1999). This is the most complete iconographic guide to medieval fox imagery. It concentrates on English material but always offers information on Continental equivalents.

Martin Wallen, *Fox* (London: Reaktion Books, 2006). Wallen's book resembles this one but has a wider scope. It begins with Aristotle and ends in modern times, it has more on biology and does not restrict itself to Western Europe. Beautifully illustrated.

BIBLIOGRAPHY

Alexander, Dominic, *Saints and Animals in the Middle Ages* (Wood-bridge: The Boydell Press, 2008).

Baillie-Grohman, William A., and Florence (eds), *The Master of Game, by Edward, Second Duke of York: The Oldest English Book of Hunting*, 2nd edn (London: Chatto & Windus, 1909).

Batany, Jean, *Scène et coulisses du 'Roman de Renart'* (Paris: Sedes, 1989).

Beer, Jeanette, 'Clergie? Chevalerie? Renardie? *Le Bestiaire d'amour* and a Woman's Response', in Adrian P. Tudor and Alan Hindley (eds), *Grant Risee? The Medieval Comic Presence. La Présence comique médiévale: Essays in Memory of Brian J. Levy* (Turnhout: Brepols, 2006), pp. 337–46.

Bellon, Roger, 'Une creation originale: la fame Renart ou le personage d'Hermeline dans le *Roman de Renart*', *Reinardus*, special volume (1993), pp. 13–29.

Bennett, J. A. W., and G. V. Smithers (eds), *Early Middle English Verse and Prose* (Oxford: Clarendon Press, 1966) (2nd edn, 1968).

Best, Thomas W., *Reynard the Fox* (Boston MA: Twayne Publishers, 1983).

Bianciotto, Gabriel (ed.), *Bestiaires du Moyen Age* (Paris: Stock, 1980).

Binkley, Peter (ed.), *Pre-Modern Encyclopaedic Texts: Proceedings of the Second COMERS Congress, Groningen, 1–4 July 1996* (Leiden: Brill, 1997).

Bodemann, Ulrike, 'Speculum sapientiae', in Kurt Ruh (ed.), *Verfasserlexikon. Die deutsche Literatur des Mittelalters*, vol. 9 (Berlin: Walter de Gruyter, 2012), pp. 65–7.

Bouwman, André, and Bart Besamusca (eds), *Of Reynaert the Fox: text and facing translation of the Middle Dutch beast epic 'Van den vos Reynaerde'*; edited with an introduction, notes and glossary and translated by Thea Summerfield; includes a chapter on Middle Dutch by Matthias Hüning and Ulrike Vogl (Amsterdam: Amsterdam University Press, 2009), open access, *www.jstor.org/stable/j.ctt46mwgf* (last accessed 20 May 2022).

Clark, Willene B. (ed.), *A Medieval Book of Beasts: The Second-Family Bestiary: Commentary, Art, Text and Translation* (Woodbridge: The Boydell Press, 2006).

Cummins, John, *The Hound and the Hawk: The Art of Medieval Hunting* (London: Phoenix Press, 1988).

Dalby, David, *Lexicon of the Medieval German Hunt* (Berlin: De Gruyter, 1965).

Darilek, Marion, *Füchsische Desintegration. Studien zum Reinhart Fuchs im Vergleich zum Roman de Renart* (Heidelberg: Universitätsverlag Winter, 2020).

Delort, Robert, *Le commerce des fourrures en occident à la fin du moyen âge (vers 1300 – vers 1450)*, 2 vols (Rome: École Française de Rome, 1978).

Dicke, Gerd, and Klaus Grubmüller, *Die Fabeln des Mittelalters und der frühen Neuzeit. Ein Katalog der deutschen Versionen und ihrer lateinischen Entsprechungen* (München: Wilhelm Fink Verlag, 1987).

Ducos, Joëlle (ed.), *Encyclopédie médiévale et langues européennes: Réception et diffusion du De proprietatibus rerum de Barthélemy l'Anglais dans les langues vernaculaires* (Paris: Honoré Champion, 2014).

Flinn, John, *Le Roman de Renart dans la littérature française et dans les littératures étrangères au Moyen Âge* (Toronto: University of Toronto Press, 1963).

Foulet, Lucien, *Le Roman de Renart* (Paris: Champion, 1914; several reprints).

Gopen, George D. (ed.), *Robert Henryson, Moral Fables* (Notre Dame IN: University of Notre Dame Press, 1987).

Göttert, Karl-Heinz (ed. and trans.), Heinrich der Glîchezâre, *Reinhart Fuchs. Mittelhochdeutsch/Neuhochdeutsch* (Stuttgart: Reclam, 1976).

Houtsma, Jos, 'Zeven Italiaanse vossen', *Tiecelijn*, 33, Jaarboek 13 (2020), 237–44.

Jacobs, John C. (ed.), *The Fables of Odo of Cheriton* (Syracuse NY: Syracuse University Press, 1985).

Jung, Marc-René, 'Epische Formen in Frankreich. Der "Roman de Renart"', in *Neues Handbuch der Literaturwissenschaft*, vol. 7: Henning Krauß (ed.), *Europäisches Hochmittelalter* (Wiesbaden: Akademische Verlagsgesellschaft Athenaion, 1981), pp. 413–21, 423–4.

Kelly, Tasha Dandelion, *A fur primer for 14th and 15th century European clothing*, *http://cottesimple.com/articles/fur-primer/* (last accessed 21 May 2022).

Librová, Bohdana, 'Le renard dans le *cubiculum taxi*: les avatars d'un exemplum et le symbolisme du blaireau', *Le Moyen Âge*, 109 (2003), 79–111.

Liere, Frans van, *An Introduction to the Medieval Bible* (Cambridge: Cambridge University Press, 2014).

Mac Coitir, Niall, *Ireland's Animals* (Cork: The Collins Press: 2010 (2nd edn, 2015)).

Mann, Jill, *From Aesop to Reynard: Beast Literature in Medieval Britain* (Oxford: Oxford University Press, 2009).

Mann, Jill (ed. and trans.), *Ysengrimus* (Cambridge MA and London: Harvard University Press 2013).

Medieval Bestiary: Animals in the Middle Ages, www.bestiary.ca (last accessed 18 May 2022).

Meier, Christel, 'Tendenzen der neueren Forschung zur Enzyklopädie des Mittelalters, in Amand Berteloot and Dieter Hellfaier (eds), *Jacob van Maerlants 'Der naturen bloeme' und das Umfeld. Vorläufer – Redaktionen – Rezeption* (Münster: Waxmann, 2001), pp. 29–47.

Menke, Hubertus, *Bibliotheca Reinardiana. Teil I: Die europäischen Reineke-Fuchs-Drucke bis zum Jahre 1800* (Stuttgart: Hauswedel & Co., 1992).

Morrison, Elisabeth, and Larissa Grollemond (eds), *Book of Beasts: The Bestiary in the Medieval World* (Los Angeles CA: J. Paul Getty Museum, 2019).

Owen, D. D. R. (trans.), *The Romance of Reynard the Fox* (Oxford and New York: Oxford University Press, 1994). Cf., *https://archive.org/details/romanceofreynard00* (last accessed 20 May 2022).

Poole, Kristopher, 'Foxes and Badgers in Anglo-Saxon Life and Landscape', *Archeological Journal*, 172(2) (2015), 389–422.

Raynaud, Gaston, and Henri Lemaître (eds), *Le Roman de Renart le Contrefait* (Genève: Slatkine, 1975; reprint of Paris edn 1914).

Regalado, Nancy Freeman, 'Tristan and Renart: Two Tricksters', *L'Esprit créateur*, 16 (1976), 30–38.

Regalado, Nancy Freeman, 'Staging the *Roman de Renart*: Medieval Theater and the Diffusion of Political Concerns into Popular Culture', *Mediaevalia*, 18 (1995), 111–41.

Rodin, Kerstin, *Räven predikar för Gässen. En studie av ett ordspråk i senmedeltida ikonografi* (Stockholm: Almqvist & Wiksell, 1983).

Roosen, Rolf ,'"Fuchshoden machet diejenigen hurtig, so sich der Weiber nicht gebrauchen können." Der Rotfuchs, ein Parforceritt durch Bibel, Tierepos und Fachliteratur', Log. Zeitschrift für internationale Literatur, 53 (2010), 175–88.

Scheidegger, Jean R., 'Renart et Arthur à la cathédrale de Modène', in Varty, À la recherche du Roman de Renart, II, pp. 391–414.

Smets, An, and Baudouin van den Abeele, 'Medieval Hunting', in Birgitte Resl, A Cultural History of Animals in the Medieval Age (Oxford and New York: Berg, 2007; reprint 2011), pp. 59–79.

Smith, Pamela H., 'Making as Knowing: Craft as Natural Philosophy', in Pamela H. Smith, Amy R. W. Meyers and Harold Cook (eds), Ways of Making and Knowing (Ann Arbor MI: University of Michigan Press, 2014), pp. 17–47.

Spiegel, Harriet (ed. and trans.), Marie de France, Fables (Toronto, Buffalo and London: University of Toronto Press: 1987).

Strubel, Armand and others (eds), Le Roman de Renart (Paris: Gallimard, 1998).

Suomela-Härmä, Elina, Les structures narratives dans le Roman de Renart (Helsinki: Suomalainen Tiedeakatemia, 1981).

Tilander, Gunnar (ed.), Les livres du roy Modus et de la royne Ratio, publiés avec introduction, notes et glossaire par, 2 vols (Paris: Société des anciens textes français, 1932).

Tilander, Gunnar (ed.), Gaston Phébus, Livre de chasse, édité avec introduction, glossaire et reproduction des 87 miniatures du manuscrit 616 de la Bibliothèque nationale de Paris par – (Karlshamn: Johansson, 1971; reprint: 1976; Graz: Akad. Druck- und Verlagsanstalt, 1994).

Trachsler, Richard, 'Renart als "Demiourgos". Tierfabel und Weltordnung im "Renart le Contrefait"', in Kathrin Lukaschek, Michael Waltenberger and Maximilian Wick (eds), Die Zeit der sprachbegabten Tiere. Ordnung, Varianz und Geschichtlichkeit (in)

der Tierepik, Beiträge zur mediävistischen Erzählforschung, Themen-heft 11 (2022), 225–52. *https://ojs.uni-oldenburg.de/ojs/index.php/bme/issue/view/*19 (accessed 14 November 2022).

Varty, Kenneth (ed.), À *la recherche du Roman de Renart*, 2 vols (New Alyth: Lochee Publications, 1991).

Varty, Kenneth, 'La mosaïque de Lescar et la datation des contes de Renart le goupil', in Varty, À *la recherche du Roman de Renart*, II, pp. 318–29.

Varty, Kenneth, 'Le goupil des bestiaries dans le Roman de Renart', in Varty, À *la recherche du Roman de Renart*, II, pp. 344–60.

Varty, Kenneth, 'Les Funérailles de Renart le goupil', in Varty, À *la recherche du Roman de Renart*, II, pp. 361–90.

Varty, Kenneth, 'Playing Dead: the Bestiary Fox on Misericords and in the *Roman de Renart*', in Paul Hardwick (ed.), *The Playful Middle Ages: Meanings of Play and Plays of Meaning: Essays in Memory of Elaine C. Block* (Turnhout: Brepols, 2010), pp. 233–44.

Varty, Kenneth, *Reynard the Fox: A Study of the Fox in Medieval English Art* (Leicester: Leicester University Press, 1967).

Varty, Kenneth, *Reynard, Renart, Reinaert, and Other Foxes in Medieval England: The Iconographic Evidence* (Amsterdam: Amsterdam University Press, 1999).

Varty, Kenneth, 'The Fox and the Wolf in the Well: the Metamorphoses of a Comic Motif', in Kenneth Varty (ed.), *Reynard the Fox: Social Engagement and Cultural Metamorphoses in the Beast Epic from the Middle Ages to the Present* (New York and Oxford: Berghahn, 2000), pp. 245–56.

Varty, Kenneth, *The Roman de Renart: A Guide to Scholarly Work* (Lanham MD and London: The Scarecrow Press, 1998).

Varty, Kenneth and Paul Wackers, 'A Selective Survey of Visual Representations of Reynardian Literature and Fox Lore in the Last Fifty Years', *Reinardus*, 30 (2018), 212–58.

Veale, Elspeth, *The English Fur Trade in the Later Middle Ages*, 2nd edn (Oxford: Oxford University Press, 1966).

Vulpes vulpes: Red fox, https://animaldiversity.org/accounts/Vulpes_vulpes/ (last accessed 20 May 2022).

Wackers, P. W. M., *De waarheid als leugen. Een interpretatie van Reynaerts historie* (Utrecht: HES, 1986).

Wackers Paul (ed.), *Reynaert in tweevoud: Deel II. Reynaerts historie* (Amsterdam: Bert Bakker, 2002).

Wackers, Paul, 'Reynard the Fox', in Willem P. Gerritsen and Anthony G. van Melle (eds), *A Dictionary of Medieval Heroes. Characters in Medieval Narrative Traditions and Their Afterlife in Literature, Theatre and the Visual Arts*, trans. Tanis Guest (Woodbridge: The Boydell Press, 1998), pp. 211–19.

Wackers, Paul, 'The Image of the Fox in Middle Dutch Literature', *The Fox and Other Animals: Reinardus*, special volume (1993), 181–98.

Wackers, Paul, 'The Printed Dutch Reynaert Tradition: From the Fifteenth to the Nineteenth Century', in: Kenneth Varty (ed.), *Reynard the Fox: Social Engagement and Cultural Metamorphoses in the Beast Epic from the Middle Ages to the present* (New York and Oxford: Berghahn, 2000), pp. 73–103.

Wallen, Martin, *Fox* (London: Reaktion Books, 2006).

Williams, Alison, *Tricksters and Pranksters: Roguery in French and German Literature of the Middle Ages and the Renaissance* (Amsterdam and Atlanta GA: Rodopi, 2000).

Williams, Alison, 'Courtly Lady, Starving Spouse and Partner in Crime: the Shifting Roles of Hermeline in the Roman de Renart', *Nottingham French Studies*, 46 (2007), 1–16.

Ziolkowski, Jan, *Talking Animals: Medieval Latin Beast Poetry, 750–1150* (Philadelphia PA: University of Pennsylvania Press, 1993).

INDEX